D1382616

Breaking Up without Cracking Up

REDUCING THE PAIN OF SEPARATION AND DIVORCE

Christopher Compston

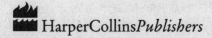

HarperCollins*Publishers*

HarperCollins*Publishers*
77–85 Fulham Palace Road, London W6 8JB

First published in Great Britain in 1998 by
HarperCollins*Publishers*

1 3 5 7 9 10 8 6 4 2

Copyright © 1998 Christopher Compston

Christopher Compston asserts the moral right to
be identified as the author of this work

A catalogue record for this book is
available from the British Library

ISBN 0 00 274001 X

Printed and bound in Great Britain by
Caledonian International Book Manufacturing Ltd, Glasgow

CONDITIONS OF SALE
This book is sold subject to the condition that it shall not,
by way of trade or otherwise, be lent, re-sold, hired out or
otherwise circulated without the publisher's prior consent
in any form of binding or cover other than that in which it
is published and without a similar condition including this
condition being imposed on the subsequent purchaser.

All rights reserved. No part of this publication may be
reproduced, stored in a retrieval system, or transmitted,
in any form or by any means, electronic, mechanical,
photocopying, recording or otherwise, without the prior
permission of the publishers.

This book is dedicated to my children
Emily, Harriet, Rupert and Benjamin Compston

And in memory of their brothers
Harry John Compston (1969)
and
Joshua Richard Compston (1970–1996)

Contents

Acknowledgements

Over the years, many people have helped me to put together this book, not that all of them know it! Family, friends, colleagues have all played their part. They are far too numerous to mention by name but thank you all the same.

I am particularly grateful to Rosemary Korbel and James Willison, stalwarts of the Divorce Recovery Seminars for many years, to Vicky Waters who allowed me to use some personal notes and who read the manuscript – and to Melanie Loram and my wife Caroline.

Melanie and Caroline deserve special mention – Melanie for typing and re-typing the manuscript with humour and patience and Caroline for unstinting support in good times and bad.

Introduction

Another book – what does he know about it anyway?

Quite a lot. Firstly, my parents divorced and I divorced. Secondly, for over 33 years, both as barrister and judge, I have been involved in hundreds of divorce cases.

Beginning with my own experiences: I was 12 when my parents divorced and I can vividly remember the unhappiness of that time, not least my father's absence, my mother's bitterness and the constant lack of money. Years later, these wounds have almost healed but some scar tissue remains.

There is nothing unique in my memories. Some years ago, a most able and sophisticated barrister was interviewed. 'Rich and glamorous, heir to a baronetcy, married to a beautiful former model, living in an exquisite country house that was open to the public.' He had this to say about his parents' separation when he was 12 and their divorce when he was 17: 'I can't say that I look upon those five years with anything but wretchedness. The impact of their leading separate lives was something which I can never forget. Today, I think of divorce as being something I could not contemplate, not just because of the anguish and misery which it would cause me and my wife but because of the sense of despair it gives a child. You can't understand why these two people you love, whom you always regarded as the bedrock of your childhood, cannot love each other or at least live in the same house. Divorce causes utter misery all round.'

When I was 28 I married a delightful girl of 19. We had a lovely house in London, a small cottage in the Isle of Wight and two splendid children. So far as I was aware we were very happily married. Then after 10 years, against my wishes, the marriage went on the rocks, ending in divorce. Many months of painful misery followed.

Secondly my professional background. I was a barrister for over 20 years and handled many divorce cases. Intellectually I could accept that people were suffering but this did not affect me emotionally one little bit until my own divorce. In a month I might handle 30 to 40 divorces, sometimes more. No details were spared. Adultery, drunkenness, violence and the like were commonplace. In addition, there were the contested cases where husband and wife were fighting over money or their children. These cases sometimes took several days, and both in and out of court you got to know the inner workings of their marriage. As a judge for over 12 years, the experience is really the same except that I am now an umpire, not an advocate. This overall view is very valuable. I should stress that the views in this book are personal, not official.

What's more, over the last 15 years, my wife and I have helped or tried to help many people who are involved in divorce and separation. We run divorce recovery seminars, the details of which appear at the end of this book.

Thus both personally and professionally, I have some experience and, although we are all unique, certain patterns of behaviour and misbehaviour emerge.

But what about separation?

To be frank, I believe that marriage is better than living together, but equally I have no doubt that the pain when people separate is just as bad as a divorce, particularly when they have been living together for a long time and have children. This book is more concerned with long-term relationships than with short affairs.

What's more, although it has taken me many years to realize this, separation can be more painful because family and friends and society in general don't rally round as much. 'After all, they never got married – it's probably all for the best.' For all its sadness, divorce has its rituals and rites of passage which, to a limited extent, cushion the blow. Separation has no rituals at all. Indeed, I well remember a friend telling me recently of her great distress when, after 10 years of living with his girlfriend, her son suddenly returned home in tears with just one small suitcase.

Of all the people we have tried to help, only one has committed suicide and she was not divorced but separated. With hindsight, none of her family or friends realized just how destroyed she was by the breakdown of her relationship. She took an overdose on Christmas Eve.

So, this book is meant to help the separated just as much as the divorced. Whenever I speak of marriage or divorce, I have you in mind as well.

A few general points may help you to get the best out of this book.

In theory, the old idea of 'innocent party' and 'guilty party' has gone, but in reality there is usually one who makes the running and delivers the final blow by continuing the adultery, the drinking, the violence or the like. So I shall refer to that person as the 'guilty' party and the one who is on the receiving end, who does not want the divorce or separation, as the 'victim' – but I should stress that this is merely short-hand. In any breakdown, both people are to blame. No one is one hundred per cent right or one hundred per cent wrong. In the history books, Richard the Lion Heart was a 'good' king and King John was a 'bad' king, but real life is more complicated. In any breakdown, both people are to blame and in a sense both are victims – although the 'winner' may not appreciate it as yet. Except in the rarest of cases, children are always victims.

A few divorces and separations are so difficult and the people involved are so difficult that even wise King Solomon would have taken a second opinion but these are rare. So beware of the cry 'No one has suffered as much as I have'. Most of us have, I promise you, but we survived and so will you. This book is intended to support and encourage.

Finally, what do I mean by helpers? Help can range from the timely cup of tea or glass of beer to in-depth counselling by professionals. It all depends upon circumstances. In our experience, many people who help have themselves suffered from divorce or separation. This is hardly surprising since only those who have gone through it can fully appreciate the hell of it. Despite this, we have been greatly helped by many others, including the unmarried, the widowed and the happily married. The most surprising people have turned out to have the right touch. What is more, most of us are surely both victim and helper at the same time. I find that the more I help or try to help the more I receive in return.

A word about anecdotes. Although I have altered the details to safeguard privacy, I can vouch for their essential accuracy. I am sure that some stories help. People are far more important (and interesting) than dry general points.

Stable
Relationships

Priorities

'There are lies, damned lies, and statistics.' I agree. However, some facts are alarming. Ruth Deech, principal of St Anne's College, Oxford, wrote in the *Daily Mail* some time ago:

The divorce rate has been running at 180,000 to 190,000 petitions a year for at least 10 years. At a modest estimate, this amounts to 3,600,000 adults experiencing divorce in the past 10 years. 1,600,000 children have grown up during their parents' divorce in the past decade.

The Times on 20 March 1996 said, 'Of current marriages, 41% are expected to break down ... England and Wales has the highest divorce rate in Europe.' In Britain, three million people will experience a broken marriage in the 1990s. One in five children can expect their parents to divorce before they reach the age of sixteen. One in seven families with dependent children have just one parent. These statistics are now so well known that there is a danger that their significance may be lost. Let's put it like this: you are one of three children, one of you will be divorced. You have three children, one of them will be divorced. You glance around the pub, the office, your family and realize that every third couple will be divorced.

Possibly you will, however unwillingly. What's more, these figures do not include separations, so the picture is really even worse.

So I make no apologies for starting this book by majoring on marriage, its priorities and its enemies. The points made are equally relevant to living together.

Firstly, prevention is better than cure. All our relationships can be improved; far better to mend and improve than pick up the pieces after irretrievable breakdown. Divorce or separation should be the last resort, not an easy first choice.

Second, just as history tends to repeat itself so do our personal histories. Our personalities can make or mar us and within a relationship they are sorely tested. In many ways, it is so much easier to be good on your own. The single often have more money, more time, more space and, above all, more sleep! Therefore, if your relationship has failed or is failing, there is a possibility that the same strains may arise in your next relationship. In short, if you have never come to terms with the failure of your first marriage or relationship or sorted out why it happened, it can cause problems in the second. Statistically, second marriages have a less than 30 per cent chance of surviving five years or more whereas third marriages have a less than 15 per cent chance. Hollywood abounds in colourful, if pathetic, examples. King Henry VIII had six wives – would you have gone to him for guidance? Or to Elizabeth Taylor?

If we begin to know ourselves and discover what went wrong before, it is less likely to occur again. Looking at our past, therefore, may well make our present and future more secure. So, even if you are divorced or your relationship seems hopelessly on the rocks, read the next chapters; they are relevant. In fact, this book should be read as a whole, with underlying themes running right through.

From a stable relationship stems the family and you will probably agree that the family is the building-block of society.

Destroy the family and you will have gone a very long way to undermining and ultimately destroying society. Those of us with large extended families, of all ages, know how valuable such families are. Admittedly families can be difficult but those who run away from them are often running away from themselves.

Nowadays the family is under attack on all sides. The result is more divorce, more one-parent families, more illegitimacy and more loneliness, especially in old age. We can see this all around. The children coming from these backgrounds may be less well equipped for later life by their lopsided start. However hard their single parents try, they have an agonizingly difficult job. Children get their first sense of values from their parents, so they are considerably disadvantaged if raised by only one. We should strive to maintain families both for our own sakes and for society's.

Our first task is to love our partner, not our parents, our children, friends. Many parents love their children more than each other. Considering how attractive young children are and how tired and tetchy we parents can sometimes be, this is understandable. We have given up everything for the kids – and the result? Often, the children either become smothered by such obsessive love that they grow up stunted and inadequate, or they just rebel. Children must be allowed to flee the nest, although our homes should always be open to them.

Finally what about work? This includes 'good works' just as much as earning your living.

Most people, with rising expenses in these difficult times, have to work very hard to earn their living and, even then, may fail to make ends meet. Both may have to go out to work, with all the attendant difficulties of getting help with the children either inside or outside the home. This puts a great strain on the relationship and on the children. A recent Gallup poll analysis showed that 90 per cent of mothers in paid employment have difficulty combining their roles. They face practical and emotional problems. Without being glib, you may well have to consider or reconsider what really matters in life. Is it promotion or is it Peter? Is it the Volvo or is it Veronica? Is it France or is it Francis? We can't take our money or our fame with us when we die.

When the American multimillionaire Rockefeller died, someone asked, 'What did he leave?', only to be given the chilling reply, 'He left everything.'

To give quality time to your partner and children may mean that you have to turn down certain offers, forgo certain opportunities, give up certain hobbies. If your job takes you constantly away from home, you may have to consider changing your job. Easier said than done, but the pressures on your health and your family's happiness may justify change.

As Rob Parsons puts it so well in his excellent book *The Sixty Minute Father*, 'No one ever said on his death bed "I wish I'd worked harder at the office!"'

Furthermore, if you stand firm, some compromise may well be reached. A director of a well-known bank in London insisted on being home in time to bath and read to his four young children. He is still a director, still has a delightful wife and the bank still prospers – unlike some! Again, we know a competent businessman who for the last 27 years has worked on four days a week. Admittedly, these examples are exceptional, but some adjustment may be possible.

The alternative is sad. Some years ago, I met the wife of a most successful barrister, a Queen's Counsel. She, her clothes and her jewellery were beautiful and she lived in one of the most expensive parts of London. Yet, after two glasses of wine, what bitterness. 'You can keep all this,' she said. 'I never see him – he never sees the children, so what's it all about?'

What indeed! He was just not at home – which brings in a further point. Whether you are working hard at the office or doing good works (for example, visiting the lonely at the local old people's home), or actually doing something wrong, it really makes little difference to your family. You were just not there when you should be.

A word about hobbies. Some hobbies are more wholesome than others but the golf widow is just as abandoned as the pub widow. We may have to tailor our hobbies to the justified needs of our wife and children.

Other relationships

Finally, we should remember other family relationships, with our parents, our brothers and sisters and other family members. When the chips are down, our family may well prove more reliable and long-term than any friend or partner.

This may not be easy; there may be many fences to mend. Our parents may have let us down; we may have let them down. If parents, we know how difficult parenting is. All the more reason for us to view our own parents' apparent failures with sympathetic understanding.

In fact, whatever our ages, they have much to teach us. The better our relationship with our parents, the better our relationship with our partner and with our own children. If one relationship is out of true, this must have a knock-on effect on the other. To make a perfect square, all four corners have to be at right angles. Particularly in the Western world, we have lost the respect due to age; society is continuing to pay a heavy price for this folly. The truth is that as we treat our parents we in turn will be treated.

There is the old legend of the young man who lived with his wife and children in a small cottage. His old father lived with them but was badly treated by both the young man and his wife, being made to sit all day on a hard wooden bench, away from the fire, in a cold corner of the kitchen. One day the man was delighted to find his young son playing with a hammer, some nails and a piece of wood. 'What are you doing, my son?' he asked. 'Making a bench for you when you are old, father,' he replied.

At the same time, we should try and be in good relationship with our brothers and sisters and wider family. They are our generation and likely to outlive our parents and, in many ways, to be more available when our children have flown the nest. I often think of two sisters, now nearly 90, whose friendship, through thick and thin, has undoubtedly enriched their lives and still does. They contrast with two sisters of similar age whose relationship, blighted with problems which began before the First World War, never resolved itself happily. What a pity.

One final word. I recently met a man who had over 100 first cousins, yet there are some with no family at all. We should 'adopt' a granny or aunt or sister. If we do, it will be a two-way traffic. We will get as much as we give.

Loneliness is dreadful – and increasing. As Mother Teresa of Calcutta said recently, 'The biggest disease today is not leprosy or tuberculosis but the feeling of being unwanted. People need to be loved; without love, people die.'

TWO

Enemies

Katharine Whitehorn, the newspaper columnist, once wrote that we should see our relationships more as fires that might need stoking rather than flames that have blown out. Wise and witty. We maintain our cars, surely we should do the same with our relationships? If only we could give them an MOT test every year. We can.

A picture may help you. View your relationship as a house. Houses need maintenance. When we marry, our house is new. Over the years, our marriage house, almost imperceptibly, settles down. It suffers from wear and tear. The odd tile comes off. The paint gets a little chipped. The carpet gets worn. Children come. Unless we are very careful, it deteriorates and can, of course, deteriorate so badly that it has to be demolished.

As a keen gardener, I prefer the picture of a garden. If you fail to take care of your garden, it soon gets out of control. For some months, I neglected my allotment. What happened? It became invaded with nettles, grass and bindweed. It took hours and hours of happy labour, ably assisted by our son Rupert, to get it back into good shape. Had we maintained it regularly, such heroic efforts would not have been needed.

Time

One of the greatest enemies of any relationship is time. How to find time, with all the other pressing demands, is very difficult indeed. Not least when so many of these demands are 'good' demands. Our parents, our children, our friends, and those in trouble all have legitimate claims upon us. When we have dealt with them and are looking forward to peace and quiet alone, what happens? So often, a child wakes, a friend telephones, a neighbour calls – yet another claim is made upon our time and the chance of quality time alone with our partner, however short, has passed. The spell of intimacy is broken and on we rush. It has been well put, 'The devil is not in a hurry, the devil is hurry.'

Faced with these challenges, a few obvious remedies come to mind. Planning helps. We plan our public life; why not plan our private life? The Americans are particularly good at this although some of their charts are a little daunting. We can plan, or at least attempt to plan, so that we have some time for each other without interruption. This can be done daily, weekly, monthly, annually. In my first marriage we didn't appreciate, let alone tackle this problem at all, so what follows is the wisdom of hindsight.

Try to have a few minutes alone with each other every day, both in the morning and in the evening.

A week can be better organized. My wife always keeps our diary ever since the occasion when we discovered that at 7 p.m. we had double booked to see different friends! Now, we try to keep an evening a week free for ourselves.

Put a sticker in the diary meaning 'no outside engagements tonight', so that you can truthfully say, 'I am sorry, we are booked that night.' A treat together once a month helps. This need not be expensive – it could be a drink in the park. The details are down to you. The principle is the point. Time for each other alone. Finally, each year, some days away are invaluable. As explained later, friends can help here.

Fun is essential. It is hard being grown up all the time. Just unwinding, temporarily shedding one's responsibilities, is essential for health and happiness. Tension can build up remorselessly unless we consciously learn to relax.

Moreover, we must take an overall view of our general situation if we are to make the best use of our time, always remembering that the good is the enemy of the best. In other words, before either of you takes on any additional activity, discuss it and agree it first. Many of us take on too much with the result that, often, these activities are not very well done. We get tired and burnt out and our home life suffers. We have to learn to say no.

A few years ago, I stupidly broke this rule by becoming treasurer to a local old people's home. It was only once a week, the home was just across the road and the old people were delightful. Yet we had too much to do anyway; I should have said no. After a few months, I dreaded the weekly visit from the warden. 'Old Annie wants to pay half cash half cheque,' 'Old Gertrude thinks you have stolen her rent,' and 'Old Alan's failing. Do you think he should go to another home?' This small duty nearly broke the camel's back. I should never have accepted. So, look at any commitment with great care. Have you the time, the skill, the energy?

Lack of communication

A second enemy is lack of communication. Some people may never have really communicated. At first they were so 'in love' that they never realized they really had very little in common. Others, when first together, communicated very well, sharing feelings all the time until, with increasing responsibilities, they communicated less and less. One train on one track became two trains on parallel tracks until the tracks began to diverge. No longer one unit but two lonely people.

Communication entails emotional communication of *feelings*, not mere thoughts. In short, both must say, 'What are my *feelings* about this or that?' WAMFA. What are my *feelings* about ... the way you drive, the way you look, the way you speak to me, the way you speak to the children? We understand with our mind. We *feel* with our heart.

People who are not prepared to communicate are the ultimate losers. In a relationship, if you can't communicate, you are in deep trouble.

Ken Crispin, an Australian lawyer, has written a most useful book, *Divorce – The Forgivable Sin?*, in which he details how a marriage can deteriorate. The first stage is the stage of erosion. During this there is a tendency to avoid confrontation, to avoid certain taboo topics. The result is the gradual but remorseless erosion of intimacy. If you are at this stage it is as well to face it bravely. If you don't, the stage of detachment will follow. By now, the walls between the two are well and truly up. There may be no open hostility. In fact, in many ways, life may be easier during this stage than during the first more painful stage of erosion. The reason is that, frankly, the people don't really care about each other at all. They are no longer one flesh but two separate beings, ripe for picking off by others. Once this stage is reached, the relationship is in very great danger. This second stage explains why people who seem to jog along quite nicely suddenly end up on the rocks. The truth is that they were living separate lives already even if they were occasionally sleeping together.

'A stitch in time saves nine.' If there is a problem, tackle it early rather than late. Going back to the picture of the house, suppose a tile came off your roof or you saw an ominous patch of fungus underneath the sink, presumably you would take action at once. A small leak can do great damage. Dry rot can spread like wildfire; it can destroy the house. Likewise, in your relationship, if there is a problem face it and face your partner with it as boldly and as lovingly as you can before it gets out of control. If I had done so in my first marriage, I wonder whether it might have been saved. As it was, I buried my head in the sand hoping the problem would go away. It didn't. Don't be an ostrich!

However painful, tackle the problem soon before it is too late. Remember that, sometimes, it is not dramatic changes that make a marriage or relationship work again but small compromises. There is the old story of the wife who complained that her husband would only make love on Sunday night which left her too tired to do the washing on Monday. The solution? Do the washing on Tuesday!

Do not let the sun go down on your anger. Try to say sorry, to forgive as soon as possible, and always by the time you go to sleep at night. This is hard – you must grit your teeth – but, ideally, over every double bed should be emblazoned, 'Do not let the sun go down on your anger.'

Keep short accounts with your partner. Don't let small tensions accumulate. Try and start every day at square one.

Other people

A third enemy to stable relationships is other people. But in most cases, if not all cases, they don't get a look in unless the relationship is already in some trouble.

Clever Charlie and drunken Dave may be as much of a danger as beautiful Belinda or handsome Harry. Aren't we all aware of amusing and attractive people, good fun but essentially un-wholesome, even dangerous? They are insidiously tempting. Far better to avoid temptation in the first place than flirt with it. In short, don't give any of them a foot in the door. This advice applies to individuals or groups: quite calmly, we have to say, 'I am not going to mix with that lot.' Again, tackle this early. Please note: this is not because we are so perfect. It is because we are so imperfect. In other words, we try to avoid temptation because we know how easy it is to fall.

Always remember that temptation is not a crime. Many, myself included, when tempted have felt guilty. The crime lies not in temptation but in feeding the temptation and giving way to it. Give the devil an inch and he will take a mile. Try and avoid taking the first steps. If you are an alcoholic don't walk home via the pub or the off-licence and certainly don't take a job in a pub!

Serious problems

But how do you cope if you are living with an alcoholic or a drug addict? Some people have serious problems.

This list is not exhaustive but would include persistent unfaithfulness, alcoholism, drugs, violence, homosexuality. In a sense, any misbehaviour should be taken seriously. However, there are major problems which we find too hard to handle alone or even with the help of a small circle of friends. These problems cannot properly be tackled here but certain guidelines may assist.

First, try to decide whether the problem is personal or stems from the relationship. Is there an underlying problem anyway? Of course, the relationship may have caused it to surface, but try to be objective. Has he always had a drink problem? Has she always been paranoid? If the answer is yes this will help you enormously. You won't feel burdened by guilt that you may have caused it and you will be better able to take proper professional advice.

Read the newspapers. Some people are habitually unfaithful. It's their problem, not yours.

Second, decide whether the problem is major or minor. Was this a one-off incident which can be handled within the relationship or was it a symptom of something far more serious, requiring professional help? It is all a matter of degree. If he returns home drunk from the office party probably you can handle it. If he pours whisky on his breakfast cornflakes, probably you can't.

Third, take the best professional advice and stick to it. Having called in the experts try and co-operate with them. If your doctor told you to lose weight otherwise you would have a heart attack, you would probably follow his advice. Likewise, if a competent adviser suggests a course of action, follow the advice. Serious problems warrant serious effort.

Finally, tell only a small circle of confidential friends and don't let them change your course of action, unless for very good reason. For instance: your partner is being unfaithful, your experienced adviser advises you to play hard to get; your best friend says, 'Oh no, fall into his arms whenever he comes home.' I don't know who is right (though I would put my money on the adviser) but I do know that, in any battle, you should have a consistent battle plan with one general in charge. Time and time again, people get advice from A, then B, and then C and wonder why they end up in a muddle. In fact, there is no right answer to their problem. A's battle strategy has good points, so has B's and so has C's. What is clear is that you cannot try all three at once.

Furthermore, even in these difficult situations, painful as they are, you and your friends should be as discreet as possible. He may be violent. She may be unfaithful. However, the children still love their parents; you may be reconciled and to harm your partner's public reputation out of temporary spite could well cause disaster, with serious consequences for you and your children.

THREE

Commitment

Many years ago, I was sitting in my garden, talking to an older married woman. She seemed old to me. In fact, she was probably 49. I will always remember her words: 'Christopher, if only you younger people knew some of the muddles and messes we got into years ago, you wouldn't be nearly so worried.' She then discussed some of our staid old neighbours and how different their lives had been 20 years before. Her clear message was persevere. Stick with it. Life isn't always a bed of roses and, from time to time, relationships are very hard work.

Lack of time, lack of communication, and other people are enemies. *The* enemy is lack of commitment. Unless you are really committed to your relationship, when problems arise, as they undoubtedly will, you may very well fail. In the end, it often comes down to staying-power, that good old-fashioned word 'guts', the guts to continue fighting even when the going is very rough indeed. Nowadays, in these days of instant results and instant gratification, people often give up without really trying.

I have never forgotten the case in which the husband and wife married on the 1st of June, and on the 2nd of June the wife went back to her mother and that was that. She never tried again. Neither did her mother try to persuade her otherwise. As the court usher so wisely said, 'If she had been my daughter, I'd have sent her back with a flea in her ear.'

You can read as many books as you like. You can go to as many doctors and therapists as you like, you can talk endlessly with your family and friends but, if you are not deeply committed to your relationship, these supports will be of little use.

Tony Parsons, writing in the *Daily Mirror* on 2 November 1995, had this to say: 'A woman will forgive a man almost anything. She will forgive infidelity, drunkenness and premature ejaculation – although probably not all on the same evening. She will forgive him if he falls asleep immediately after sex. She will forgive if he falls asleep immediately before sex. But the one thing a woman will never forgive in a man is a lack of commitment.' Rather more soberly (but the message is the same) Lady Fisher, wife of the Archbishop of Canterbury and mother of six sons, was once asked if she ever considered divorcing her husband. Her answer was robust: 'No – but I've considered murdering him several times!'

Let me come nearer to home. At the same time that my first marriage was in difficulties, so were four other marriages, with one partner having an affair on the side. All of us had young children. However, these four couples wanted their marriages to survive, partly for their own sakes and certainly for the sake of their children, and despite serious difficulties they worked at and through their problems. And, 20 years later, they are still together; they showed staying-power and it paid off.

Solving people's problems has more to do with the character of the people than the complexities of the situation.

Your relationship may be so difficult that separation is inevitable. The point I wish to stress is that any relationship requires hard work and that if you persevere you may well win through.

Furthermore, love is not dependent on feelings. Of course, feelings are very important but love must be made of sterner stuff. We may have to use our will, almost going on automatic pilot, when our feelings are at a low ebb. Hollywood and the like have done immeasurable harm in spreading the myth that love is mere candyfloss and that when the candyfloss goes then off you go too. It is nonsense.

One final point. Let's go back to our picture of the house or garden. If we were told that we could never move from either our house or our garden what would we do? Surely, if we knew that we could not move house, we would do our level best to live in it, making all necessary adaptations and alterations. If we could not move from our garden, we would have to adapt our planting to the soil and site. We may well like rhododendrons but if they won't grow in our soil then we will have to find alternatives. Surely, faced with this challenge, most of us would make an excellent job of it even if originally it was not quite what we had in mind. So persevere.

In 1996 when my mother died, I inherited her small flat in the Isle of Wight. She had lived in it alone for many years and, at first glance, it seemed quite unsuitable for our family, with a girl of 11 and two boys of eight and four. How would we all fit in? Where would we all sleep? Where would we eat, since the kitchen was so poky? And as for the garden, what would we do? The front garden was exposed to the road and quite dangerous for children and as for the back garden, what a mess! Obviously, the flat would have to be sold. On the other hand, we certainly couldn't afford to buy another flat and all of us loved visiting the Isle of Wight. So we sat down and thought it through and, after much hard work and relatively small expense, adapted the flat for family use. Faced with making the best of what we had, in other words, either keeping the flat or having no flat at all, we were able to make a go of it. It all comes down to commitment.

Incidentally, on average, marriages founder four months short of the tenth wedding anniversary. I don't know where this statistic comes from but my marriage effectively failed a few days before our tenth wedding anniversary and the legendary 'seven year itch' must have some basis in folklore. Commitment is needed throughout any relationship through to the end. Sad to say, many relationships come to grief when people retire. One reason must be that, for the first time for many years, couples have to face living together 24 hours a day.

Making it better

So, how can we help our relationship along? If we have already failed, what could we have done? The point here being not a bitter post mortem but a frank evaluation of the past so that we can have happy lives now and in the future. We may as well build on our mistakes rather than be crushed by them.

This book is not primarily concerned with saving relationships. Others with considerably more authority than I (after all, they haven't failed!) have both written and spoken wisely and well. However, the following tips may assist. These come from psychiatrist Jack Dominian, director of the marriage research charity, One Plus One. He has identified five key elements which work to maintain relationships.

1 AVAILABILITY. Each couple must discover the right balance of being together and being apart. Unemployment and excessive overtime both lead to stress.
2 COMMUNICATION. Talking and intimacy are the heart of a happy marriage.
3 AFFECTION. Regular demonstrations of affection are a must for most couples. Saying 'I love you' matters even after 30 years.

4 AFFIRMATION. Be positive about things your partner does well and appreciate them for how they are. We are familiar with the need to praise and compliment children – it is just as important for partners.
5 RESOLUTION OF CONFLICT. Contented couples don't respond to criticism with more criticism. They try to understand each other's point of view and are ready to apologize and admit responsibility.

Books

Even the most indifferent cook has some cookery books on the kitchen shelf. Others have whole libraries, not that they are necessarily the best cooks! How many of us have even one book on making a relationship work?

Two slight words of caution. First, if your relationship is in difficulties, I advise reading such books discreetly. To sit up in bed reading *How To Make Your Partner Perfect* is hardly tactful. Once you have mastered and digested the contents then share them by all means and, if the time is right, share the book as well.

Second, if you are going to lend a book, not only should you have read it but try to pick the right book. If your husband is in the army and has just come back from a commando course, he may well not get excited about a book with a bunch of daffodils on the cover. A life of Leonard Cheshire, founder of the Cheshire Homes, who won the Victoria Cross in the Second World War, may be a better bet. By the same token, a highly strung woman may well find an earthy sex manual more than she can cope with at such a time, even if it is really what she needs.

Seminars

There are some excellent seminars. I have not specifically rec-
ommended any because the details and the leaders change.
Ideally, they should be led by couples who are realistic, amusing and down to earth, preferably having many responsibilities
and their own children. Avoid those who preach at or down
to you.

Alternatively you might consider having informal seminars
of your own, covering aspects of marriage and parenthood.
These can be invaluable, not least because you know the parties concerned, both the speakers and the audience. They
should be done well or not at all.

Marriage review weekends

There are very experienced couples who run such courses and
are training others to do so. We have attended two, with considerable benefit, not that it was always easy having to face
ourselves so intimately! Although these can be comparatively
expensive, they are worth every penny. One of the great
advantages is that you are in relaxed surroundings, without
your children and with all your usual responsibilities suspen-
ded. Another advantage is that you may well find kindred
spirits with whom you can share your problems. Very often,
you are not likely to meet them again so, provided you know
what you are doing, you can probably be more open and frank
with them than you would normally be.

And what about those who are living together?

Do all these points apply? They do, but I repeat my firm view that marriage is better than living together. The very act of marriage is a public statement of commitment which is so often lacking when people are just living together. There is good evidence that couples who live together before getting married are more likely to get divorced than those who do not. Frankly, I found this statement hard to believe but I have read it so often that I am sure that it is true and, on further thought, can well understand why.

Postscript

Although this book is not primarily concerned with saving relationships, those wishing to help might consider the following points:

- In an emergency, anyone can help, but preferably consult experienced people.
- It is unwise to help the opposite sex alone.
- Two heads are often better than one. Men may well miss a clue which women pick up, and vice versa.
- Practical and financial help, especially in times of stress, may make the crucial difference. Small acts of kindness are often more valuable than big gestures.
- Always encourage.

During a Divorce
or Separation

FOUR

Is It Such a Good Idea?

This question can be asked in two ways. Legally, what is the position? Morally, what is the position? Sadly, the two do not always overlap.

The law

Legally, the answer is simple. The new divorce law, after much consideration, has altered some of the details but, essentially, if you want a divorce, you can get one. There are a few more hurdles in the way but remember, the law is not in the business of saving marriages. Once people pass through the solicitor's door, they very rarely turn back. It is downhill all the way. As a barrister, I never saw a reconciliation. As a judge, I have only annulled one divorce because of a reconciliation. Suffice it to say that, except in the rarest of circumstances, if anyone wishes to obtain a divorce, in law they can. But – and this is a big question – is this a good idea?

Should I divorce? Should I separate?

Many of us have to do so because our partners force it upon us. In other words, we are on the receiving end. All the same, as explained later, we can help to make the process rather less devastating. But what of those, either individuals or couples, who are on the brink, who are still contemplating whether to proceed or not. Only you can decide – you, not your lawyers, although some lawyers tend to forget this! In fact, sad to say, without being too cynical, some people have a vested interest in the divorce industry. You must make the decision, not them, and the step is so important and so irrevocable that, before taking it, think very carefully indeed, taking wise advice from your family or friends.

When thinking and discussing the following points should be borne well in mind. Frankly, in the cold pages of a book, it is hard to do some of them justice. Let me begin with Dr Richard Rahe of the University of Washington School of Medicine. He has produced a life change unit scale in which, after much investigation, he has awarded units to the various changes and chances which happen to all of us. Here is the chart and, at once, you will notice that divorce is the second highest at number 73.

Death of spouse	100
Divorce	73
Marital separation	65
Prison term	63
Death of close family member	53
Personal injury or illness	53
Marriage	50
Losing job	47
Marital reconciliation	45
Retirement	45

Change of health of family member	44
Pregnancy	40
Sex difficulties	39
Gain of new family member	39
Business readjustment	39
Change in financial state	38
Death of a close friend	38
Change in type of work	36
Change in number of marital arguments	35
Large mortgage or loan	31
Foreclosure of mortgage or loan	30
Change of responsibilities at work	29
Son or daughter leaving home	29
Trouble with in-laws	29
Outstanding personal achievement	28
Spouse begins or stops work	26
Begin or end school or college	26
Change in living conditions	25
Trouble with boss	20
Change in working hours	20
Change in residence	20
Change in school or college	20
Change in recreation	19
Change in church activities	18
Moderate mortgage or loan	17
Change in sleeping habits	15
Holiday	13
Christmas	12
Minor violation of the law	11

From time to time, I look at this list and still find it interesting. Why not pin it up somewhere at home or at work? At the very least, it will start a conversation! Whatever you may think of its accuracy, it certainly suggests that divorce is, as we know, a very significant event in a person's life.

Experts have suggested that divorce and separation are a process which falls into three stages. The first, acute, stage lasts about a year and we will consider this stage in this chapter. I should stress that this first stage can last longer, sometimes much longer, if no sensible agreement is reached. The second stage is transitional where people, in recovery, try to work through their experiences, possibly forming new relationships, having new jobs and moving house. This phase lasts about three and a half years and can of course be very difficult for all involved, not least the children. The final stage, after four and a half or so years, is reached when all concerned have settled down into their new lives. Having only recently discovered these ideas, I found them particularly telling because, over many years, by rule of thumb, I have suggested to people that it takes five years, from start to finish, fully to recover from a divorce or separation. However, let us return to the acute phase and see some of the many problems involved.

Pain

Separation is very painful. Usually it is most painful for the victim, though even those pressing for it will be surprised at their intermittent bouts of pain. From time to time, the pain is almost overwhelming, it is so acute. At other times, the pain is dormant but can strike without warning. Only those who have been through it can fully understand. The outsider will never fully appreciate the pain. Two pictures may help. Hans Christian Andersen retold the old legend of the mermaid who became human in order to capture the handsome prince. Every step she took on land was as if a knife was running through her body. Closer to home, when we were in pain as children we ran to our parents' arms. In a partnership, we naturally run to our partner, only to remember while running that it is the partner who is causing the pain.

As a divorce barrister, I accepted intellectually that the parties were in pain. But only when it happened to me did I begin to understand emotionally what people had been going through.

Many years ago, after my second wife had had two miscarriages, a sympathetic doctor's wife told us that even her own husband had not appreciated the pain of miscarriage until she herself had one. Then, permanently, his attitude to his patients changed. This advice had a very tragic sequel. About 10 years later, the doctor, then a father of four, had an affair with his secretary. His wife was so distressed that she stabbed the secretary to death with a kitchen knife. As her barrister said at the Old Bailey, 'This crime was born, not out of jealousy or revenge, but out of utter despair, desperation and anger. She held her husband and children as the most important features in her life.' Having admitted manslaughter, she was sent to prison for four years. That's pain for you.

Less dramatically, even after 25 years, I recall a man, as macho as they come, bursting into tears in conference at the sheer misery caused him by his partner's adultery. Not only are you in pain but so are your family who so often tend to be ignored at this stage except as a sounding board or possible retreat. But what about them? Particularly as we get older, much of our life is bound up with the happiness of our children and grandchildren.

Finally, and this can never be stressed enough, the pain caused to our children is incalculable. Even if they appear to be better off at the moment or 'not to be taking it too badly', in nearly every case they are harmed and these harmful effects can last a lifetime. Indeed it is now known that children whose parents have divorced are more likely to suffer from anorexia nervosa or bulimia. Time and time again, we meet people, including old people, still not recovered from their parents' divorce. This can be passed on to their children in turn. Not surprisingly, if you have had poor role models as parents, you are less likely to be a good role model yourself. By the same token, child abusers have often themselves been abused as children.

In March 1996, my son Joshua, aged 25, died. He was a brilliant maverick and his death hit us all very hard. I kept a journal for some months after his death and found myself writing that, for all the pain I was going through at that time, it was nothing by comparison with the pain of my divorce 16 years before. I am sure that my journal was right. In fact, having discussed this with a doctor friend who had suffered both divorce and the death of a child, he unhesitatingly agreed with me. I repeat: The pain of divorce is terrible. In its acute stage, except for rare moments, it permeates and pervades night and day.

Grief

Grief is different from pain though intimately bound up with it. If you separate, you will be involved in a grief situation just as poignant, perhaps even more so, than being widowed. It takes a long time to recover from grief. Some people never do. Well into their seventies, even eighties, they are still recounting, as yesterday, the wrongs done them nearly 50 years ago.

Depression and panic attacks can be manifestations of grief. Even if they are not, they occur, believe you me, whether you like it or not! Unfortunately, whereas the world will rally round when you are grief stricken by a death, the world will not rally round when you are grief stricken by a divorce or separation.

Guilt

If we have been the main cause of the split we should quite rightly feel ashamed because we have betrayed our relationship and betrayed our children. If we wish to be really free of this guilt, we should say sorry to our former partner. Even if years have passed, you can still do this and, perhaps, write a letter saying how sorry you are to the people you have wronged. Even if you are the victim, you may still be riddled with guilt, feeling an almost intolerable sense of failure. Intellectually, you may realize that you are far from being all to blame and your loyal family and friends will repeatedly tell you so.

But the fact remains that, emotionally, you just feel a failure all the time – and in all spheres, not just your failed relationship. This is a very heavy burden which, as detailed later, can and must be overcome if you are going to regain your health and happiness. If you are facing a separation, face the fact that you will feel guilty even if essentially you are not to blame. Many of us have found that, in a most sinister but effective way, the 'guilty' partner has managed to transfer onto us a good deal of the guilt. For instance, he effectively brought your relationship to an end by drinking to excess and beating you up. You, until you regain your senses, go around blaming yourself on the lines that you must have driven him to it. Of course, you are partly to blame, but don't let him put his guilt onto you.

Anger

You will feel very angry, particularly if you are the victim. In a way, this anger is natural and healthy. It has a purpose. It may well be an important driving force for many people.

Anger, if handled well and ultimately overcome, can both refine and strengthen you. You will have to work through it. Anger must be resolved if we are to find the energy to rebuild our lives. Sharing your anger with loyal friends can help provided you do not ask too much of them. Alternatively, why not follow two other useful tips? Why not focus on something rather than someone? In other words, go and dig the garden, pulling out the weeds (your partner!), thereby getting your own back; or clear out a cupboard, putting out all the rubbish (your partner!) into the waste bin.

Many years ago, at home in the Isle of Wight, we had a wooden lavatory seat and my mother, when aroused, would robustly repaint it. This method had drawbacks if you were not warned. Physical exercise is another excellent way of releasing tension. Hang the weather, the lawyers, the bills and your partner, get up now and have a brisk walk.

In May 1992 the world delighted, for a few hours, in the antics of Lady Moon, the estranged wife of the fifth baronet, Sir Peter Graham-Moon. 'To relieve intense hurt and frustration', as she put it, she snipped the sleeves off her husband's Savile Row suits, daubed his BMW motorcar with paint and deposited his vintage wines on the village doorsteps, thereby causing about £30,000 worth of damage. My first reaction was sympathetic. She had apparently had a raw deal and why not get her own back? My second reaction was a little more judicial. She committed various criminal offences, cost the family a good deal of money and doubtless caused her sons considerable embarrassment. On balance, it was probably not very wise.

A more recent case described in *The Times* on 24 June 1997 is equally entertaining. When an enraged husband found the lodger in bed with his wife, he was so angry that he tipped six black bags full of the lovers' clothes into a cesspit. He had been married to his wife for 25 years. They had three children and as his defending advocate rightly said, 'There is no greater provocation for a man than to find his wife's lover living under the same roof.' At the magistrates' court, the husband admitted criminal·damage and the magistrates, very wisely, gave him a conditional discharge for 12 months. As with Lady Moon, I fully sympathize with the husband but his action was not very wise.

It is better to develop a technique of letting out your anger without harming either yourself or anyone else. At one of our seminars, we were delighted with a cosy middle-aged lady whose husband had run off with a younger woman. Whenever she got angry, she used to put her husband's photograph on the sofa and throw cushions at it across the room until she felt better. In the obituary of George Beeby, a distinguished business man, it was said that 'he remained volatile in temperament but his well known outbursts of indignation were soon over. His secretary used to keep a drawer for angry letters he asked her to post and regretted the following day.'

From time to time, I have written angry letters but, except on one occasion which I partly regret, have never sent them. It's down to you to find a safe method of releasing your anger. Be honest about your anger, release your anger but, for goodness sake, don't be angry for ever. It won't help you one little bit.

Therefore, realize that you will be angry but, if you can, avoid letting anger harm either you or others. Do nothing irrevocable.

Loneliness

If you have been reasonably happy together you will be very lonely at this time. Moreover, even those who wanted the separation will, at times, feel lonely if they have any conscience.

Both of you can lessen some of this inner loneliness by outside activities but lonely you will undoubtedly be. One writer has talked of a 'deep and pervasive feeling of loneliness – the loneliness cuts like a knife. It twists and turns and the pain can be relentless and unbearable, both for the one who left and the one who remains.' Even with a new lover, you can still feel lonely. In *The Times* of 2 December 1994, quoting from some studies written up in the *British Medical Journal*, the health correspondent said, 'loneliness kills more people than cancer or heart disease'.

Pausing there, let me introduce 'Frantic Fred' and 'Forlorn Freda' or, if you prefer the Mr Men books, Mr Frenzy and Miss Slump. They are both victims of loneliness. Fred spends all his waking moments doing things in a desperate effort to avoid facing his loneliness. Freda, equally tormented, does nothing at all, being almost drowned in depression. Both characters are to be pitied and, to some extent, you will be one or the other, sometimes both on the same day.

Incidentally, you may well find as I did that you will be willing to alter your value system, your general code of behaviour, because you rashly and wrongly think that such a change will bring you relief. You start to drink or smoke too much, mix with the wrong company, even sleep around. This may bring relief in the short run but in the long run, it will not. Fortunately, I found that this phase passed quite quickly.

Financial

You cannot cut the cake into two parts of equal size. Unless you are extremely rich a split leads to financial problems, often very damaging financial problems. This is hardly surprising. Lawyers, estate agents, sometimes doctors and psychiatrists get involved and have to be paid. Usually the family home has to be sold and one parent with the children rehoused in poor-er accommodation. If employed, your firm may be prepared to carry you for a while even if you do have days off, but if you are self-employed you will just lose that day's income.

As a rule of thumb, I endorse a friend who said that his divorce set him back ten years. At 45 and with many responsi-bilities, he had the status and income of a 35-year-old, having dropped so many rungs on the work ladder. He could never regain those lost rungs. As an American put it, 'Financial life after divorce is the pits!' In my own case, despite much family financial support and an excellent job, I still find it quite hard to make ends meet. Why? mainly because, at the age of 43, to a large extent I had to start financially all over again and a new wife and three young children, delightful as they are, do not come cheap.

You must appreciate that, if you divorce or separate, you may well have acute financial problems, possibly for the rest of your life. What's more, the lawyers, the accountants, the estate agents will all take their slice of the cake so when you and your partner come to divide it there will be a smaller cake anyway. It is beyond the scope of this book, but there is over-whelming proof of the close relationship between single par-enthood and being poor.

Divorce is not a final solution

Finally, remember that unless yours is a short relationship, with no children, separation is not a final solution. It is a solu-tion of sorts in that you are free to find someone else but you may still have financial responsibilities towards your former partner and you will undoubtedly have emotional and finan-cial responsibilities towards your children. These will not go away for many years. What is more, as your children grow up you will have to face school functions and weddings and, when they have children, there will be christenings and parties and the like and sometimes family tragedy. Death is final: divorce and separation are not. Opinions may vary but in my view, the death of a partner may be less traumatic in the long run than divorce or separation. There are two reasons for this. Firstly, death is a full stop. It's all over. Secondly, society rallies round when somebody dies and it doesn't when somebody is divorced or separated.

Divorce or separation is not an event but a process. This needs explanation. If you go to an event such as a dance or a football match, its after-effects are minimal (unless you are Cinderella!). Once the event is over, that's it. A divorce is totally different. You get your divorce on a certain date which has some legal and financial implications but afterwards there is still a long process of adjustment. This normally becomes less intense over the years but, in a sense, the after-effects of divorce are lifelong. Hence, divorce is not an event but a process.

Children

Your children will be hurt. No question of it. Your children will be hurt. Cardinal Daly of Ireland has rightly referred to children under these circumstances as 'the orphans of living parents'. A separation is always painful for children, whatever their ages. For many years, I believed that provided parents stuck together until the children left school then, all in all, 'it wasn't too bad'. I now believe that nearly all children are hurt, however old they are, and hurt badly even if, as adults, they are able to disguise their hurt quite well.

At the present moment, we know of two people, one 24 and one 30, who are devastated (there is no other word) by the separation of their parents. For my own part, when I consider how essential my parents-in-law are both to our happiness and that of our children, I just can't imagine how dreadful we would find it if they were to separate – which, mercifully, seems quite out of the question. They have been happily married for well over 50 years.

Thinking deeply about this, I wonder whether this analogy helps? When a child dies, however old, no one dares to suggest to the grieving parents that their grief is any the less because the child was 30 or even 40 or 50. Why should it be any less painful the other way round?

As reported in *The Times* of 2 May 1995, Dr Martin Richards, who runs the Centre for Family Research at Cambridge University, is an expert on divorce. He and his colleagues studied 17,000 children who were born in Britain during one week in 1958 and were followed up at the ages of seven, 11, 16 and 23. He wrote, 'As a university teacher I see that even when children have left home and are in their early twenties, their parents' separation or divorce can be very disturbing for them. Adolescents are particularly vulnerable, probably for similar reasons; at a point when they are learning about relationships, they see the most important relationship in their lives fall apart.'

He also discovered that children survive best where good contact is maintained with both the parents, a point we will explore later. But for the moment you must face that if you divorce or separate, your children's loss of trust and faith in you is inevitable because you have let them down. Two thirds of people involved in divorce have children and it is now generally accepted that children are usually far better off when their parents stay together, however unhappily, than when they divorce or separate. They are the innocent victims.

Tragically, divorce and separation still tend to focus on the needs and rights of the adults far more than on the children (although not as much as before) and parents are often in such pain that, at this most crucial stage, they are in no position properly to help their children through their pain. This pain is felt in two ways. Firstly, children are bewildered, even battered by what is happening to them. It hurts like hell. They love both parents: think how awful it must be to see those parents being nasty to each other – sometimes in violence, sometimes without violence. In fact, I sometimes think that non-violent hatred between parents can be even crueller to children than actual violence. It is more insidious, more controlled and just as horrible.

Secondly, even if the children are not in pain or say that they're not in pain, they are nevertheless damaged by their parents' separation. At first, life may be a little easier. After all, the fighting has stopped – but if they live with one parent and have limited or no contact with the other, they can grow up lopsided, with no knowledge of normal family life, warts and all.

A word of encouragement

These points are grim and well worth taking very seriously indeed. But don't despair, the remaining chapters are meant to assist and encourage you. You are about to embark on a perilous voyage with stormy seas, violent winds and hidden rocks and currents but you can reach safe harbour in the end. You cannot change the facts but you can change your attitude to them.

FIVE

Professional Help

The runaway train went over the hill and she blew,
blew, blew, blew, blew,

Once proceedings begin they are very hard to stop. They develop their own momentum; it is downhill all the way. So, before you begin, think over all the difficulties long and hard. Ask yourself, 'Have I really done all I can? Have I really put the children first? All in all, won't I be worse off at the end of the day?'

Attitude

Be positive.

If separation is inevitable, your attitude during the process can still make a considerable difference. Compare the finesse of a surgical operation to the dismembering of cattle in a slaughterhouse. As a student, I spent a year in the Argentine and, in Patagonia, visited a slaughterhouse where the sheep were driven in from the plains at one end and, in a remarkably short time, their bits and pieces came out the other end. It was a ruthless, bloody, messy business. A surgical operation requires infinite skill and patience. Are you going to be a surgeon or a butcher? Are you going to employ a surgeon or a butcher? Even if your relationship is irretrievably on the rocks, it is still a vital relationship. It still has some life in it so, clearly, a surgeon is better than a butcher.

If you view your relationship as a house you are now faced with the problem of dismantling your house, of literally pulling it down. You can either do this carefully, with as little damage to you and your children as possible, or you can knock it down with a ball and chain. Which is better? If you are pressing for a split you can set the tone of the whole proceeding. Even if you do not want this to happen, your attitude and your reactions can usually still have considerable impact. The main difficulty is that you are called upon to be fair and reasonable when your life is in ruins and you are pressed on all sides.

Solicitors

If you have only been married or living together a short time, have very few assets and no children, you may well not need a solicitor. Normally, a solicitor's help is required. You should choose your solicitor with great care. The family solicitor who dealt with Granny's will or that nice young man who conveyed your flat four years ago may well not be the answer: their expertise does not lie in divorce. Clearly, you require an experienced solicitor but there is more to it than that. Personalities matter. You should not choose the most sympathetic solicitor nor the most aggressive. Why not? If they are too sympathetic then, when the crunch comes, they may well not be able to take a wholly professional, independent and objective view. On the other hand, if they are too aggressive then you may well find yourself plunged into expensive litigation when a more sensible and tolerant approach would have settled the matter, at less cost and less pain to all concerned.

Above all, you must respect your solicitor and your solicitor must respect you. In my own divorce, I well remember on one memorable occasion my solicitor standing up to me and telling me not to be a fool. He was quite right and, with a gulp, I took his advice. Your self-respect is low at this time but you are the client and, as such, you are entitled to have your case done your way. On the other hand, in many ways you are in a patient/doctor relationship, so you need to rely on somebody who, if the occasion warrants it, is able to stand up to you. There is little point in going to your doctor and asking for advice if you don't follow that advice. If you are grossly overweight and told to eat less, then eat less. Surely your doctor is entitled gently to tick you off if, on your next visit, you haven't done what you were told. It should be just the same with your solicitor.

There is a wise old saying that 'a lawyer who acts for himself has a fool for a client'. How true this is. I know many lawyers, wisdom personified on the bench or at the bar (or at least they think so), but whose private decisions are sometimes amazingly silly. No doubt I am the same. So you need a solicitor who looks at the matter in the round, is fair and objective and deserves your respect. Above all find an experienced, competent solicitor of integrity who is on your wavelength. If your solicitor suggests a counsellor first, follow that advice.

Most solicitors and barristers are very sound and, in family matters, have no wish unnecessarily to run up costs. However, there are exceptions. Beware. I well remember trying a case, with expensive solicitors and expensive barristers. There were files galore, hundreds of pages of exhibits and the case took some days. It should have been settled, in other words agreed between the parties. Alternatively, it could and should have been tried in one day. As it was, so much money was spent in costs that, in the end, there was really very little left to rehouse one of the parents, let alone provide reasonable maintenance for the children – quite disgraceful.

On an even more personal note, some years ago we tried to help a wife who, on any view, was having an appalling time with her husband. She had an open and shut case. She had very little private money and went to a solicitor who asked her for £10,000 on account, although this would have effectively wiped out all her assets. She came to us in great distress. Within a week, I had found her a solicitor, just as competent, who, rather diffidently, asked for a down payment of £200! Furthermore, he handled her situation so skilfully that against the odds, she and her husband and the three children are still together. All may not be perfect between them but they are surviving. I have no doubt whatsoever that had the first solicitor had the conduct of the case they would have been divorced years ago.

Of course, sometimes you have to go to court but normally, experienced lawyers can avoid this. If you have very little money, legal aid may help you, but please note that nowadays, quite understandably, the Legal Aid Fund have the first rights on the family money once all the litigation is over. Time and time again, one finds what little money there was wasted, squandered, on fighting the case.

By far the best course is to ask around your friends and acquaintances who have recently been through a divorce or separation and choose your solicitor accordingly. Then, try like mad to agree or, at the very least, limit the areas of disagreement.

Counsellors

The word 'counsellor' sounds formidable. Helper may be a better word. A counsellor can range from a good friend right up to a professionally qualified psychiatrist. Fortunately most of us will not require such qualified help. If you do, then follow the general approach suggested for solicitors and, except in the rarest of circumstances, once you have found your expert stick with that person. Here we are more concerned with the middle range of helper. Some helpers may have no training at all whereas others may have had some training from an organization such as Relate, or may have taken a course. Experience, maturity, common sense count but so does training; ideally, try and find a counsellor with both. You are vulnerable and there are fakes and charlatans around.

Incidentally, sometimes I come across people who are constantly changing their solicitors. There may be good reasons but, generally speaking, there aren't. I would go further. Most lawyers would accept that one change of solicitor may be justified, but if a person is on to their third or fourth solicitor this raises serious doubts. It probably means that the client has not co-operated with the earlier solicitors or has, stubbornly and stupidly, refused to accept their sound advice. Likewise, people who constantly change their advisers are not doing themselves much good. For one thing, it may suggest that they are not able to take sound advice. For another, confusion may well occur. As with any problem, you must have a consistent strategy.

This consistent strategy point is very important. Let us go back to the house picture. If you wish to paint the outside of the house white and your partner wishes to paint the outside of the house red, one of you will have to give way because, on any view, a house half white and half red would look both ugly and absurd. The same goes for advice. If one adviser suggests that you write a friendly letter to your partner who has deserted you, whereas another adviser says 'Write as tough a letter as you reasonably can,' who is right? There are probably good reasons either way but one thing is clear – you must decide on a course of action and stick to it. What's more, even when the case is in court, it is essential that you know what you want to happen, in other words that you have a ground plan. If you don't, everyone involved, not least the vulnerable children, will be confused.

A few obvious points: as with solicitors, you must respect your counsellor. From time to time, the advice may be hard to swallow. You are not a child and the pill cannot always be sugar-coated, but if you respect your counsellor you are more likely to do what you are told. Usually, your counsellor should be your age or older. Not that we all get wiser with age – far from it! All the same, if you are 40, coping with three children and an unfaithful husband, you may well find the well-meaning advice of an unmarried 23-year-old verging on the unrealistic, however well qualified they are on paper.

Normally, your counsellor should be of the same sex, otherwise there is a danger of emotional involvement which will damage you both. You may prefer to have counselling with a couple, sometimes married, sometimes not. Sadly, in some situations, you may not be able to have any counselling at all, hence the justification for this and other books. We have found that two minds are often better than one and what shocks my wife bores me, whereas she rightly sees significance in something which I have dismissed as trivial. Only a few weeks ago an acquaintance casually said six words to us. My wife found them more revealing than all that had been said over the preceding weeks. Later events have conclusively proved her to be right.

You can counsel anywhere, at any time. You may be chatting in the launderette or outside school or doing the washing up or walking along the beach. The formal 'headmaster's study' approach may well be very off-putting although, undoubtedly, there are times when this is the only way to bring matters to a head. May I stress that, as a counsellor, you should always ask yourself, 'Am I up to this?' If we cannot cope, the sooner we transfer the person to someone who can the better. Better for us and better for them.

Friends

Most of us, fortunately, do not need counsellors at all. We merely need friends. When trouble strikes, you will find that not all your old friends remain loyal. Some desert you out of embarrassment, the sheer inability to cope with their own emotions let alone yours. Others desert you for worse reasons. You are no longer as rich and successful or as much fun as you were before and they move on to richer pickings which may include your former partner. Either way, forget these people. There is no point in being bitter and, as a wise old friend told me during my divorce, far better to be shot of people like that if they are going to let you down in your hour of need. Your closest friends may not turn up trumps. However, contrast their disloyalty with the surprising and encouraging love and loyalty shown you by lesser friends or by people you have never met before. In retrospect, I find that although I was hurt by the behaviour of some fair-weather friends, I can truly say that their loss was ultimately minimal. Moreover, far finer friends have replaced them.

Looking back over the years, in a kinder light, I have to say that with the exception of one couple whose behaviour was mean, even cruel, I now have no quarrel at all with the rest of our friends who 'sided' with my wife. They had their reasons, good reasons. They have always been pleasant and kindly whenever we have met. There is no point at all in looking back and feeling bitter and resentful. Move on and make new friends.

During the actual break-up try to surround yourself with a small, loyal circle of friends, choosing them for their loyalty, their love and – dare I say it – their laughter. Incidentally, they may well find that you are talking at them rather than talking to them but, for a while, they will just have to put up with that! Keep your gloomy friends for when you are feeling stronger. All of us have friends and relations who are heavy going. Don't drop them all together at this time, but you would be wise to 'put them on the back-boiler' until you are feeling more able to cope. If you have few friends or have recently moved to a new area, at least try to find someone, always avoiding emotional entanglements.

Chad Varah founded the Samaritans in 1953. They assist those contemplating suicide, often by just listening to them on the telephone. It is now a large international organization, dealing with millions of calls each year in the United Kingdom. When asked about volunteers, he had this to say: 'I would not have anyone who was prudish or preachy because the prudish want to sit in judgment and reject, which could drive people to suicide; the preachy want to talk instead of listen, they will not accept the person as he or she is.' He went on to say that the qualities he looked for were based on how he imagined he would feel if he were burdened with guilt or extreme unhappiness when facing that person. 'I ask myself: Could I tell it to that face?' (*Independent*, 30 April 1992).

Choose, if you can, that type of person for your small circle and within this small circle, be yourself. Tell them your pains and your pleasures without demanding more of them than they are able to give.

True friends?

Having built up your small circle of friends, always beware of false friends and acquaintances. You may well not have known them before and, if in good health and happiness, would have avoided them. Many of us can confirm that, in these times of crisis, such people come out of the woodwork, noting your weakness, seeing what they can get out of it. Usually in a mess themselves, they may seek your time, your money, your body. In conversation, I have sometimes referred to these people as vipers or piranha fish. They are in all walks of life, out for all they can get.

Well over 40 years ago, when my mother was trying to cope on her own, I recall that she was swindled out of £100 by a smooth talking confidence trickster whose face (and charm) I will never forget.

You are in no position to cope with such people so please don't give them an inch. If in doubt, ask your true friends. At this difficult time, your powers of discernment are not at their best: all the more reason to trust your true friends' advice.

It is very tempting to tell the world, particularly if you have been wronged. This temptation is almost overwhelming. Resist this temptation. There are many reasons why you should. First, you may reconcile. Second, badly as your partner has behaved, that person is still the parent of your children. Third, your complaints, even if justified, don't do your reputation any good. The truth will out. You don't have to shout it from the hilltops.

SIX

First Aid When the Crunch Comes

Edward Lear wrote,

> *The Owl and the Pussy-cat went to sea,*
> *In a beautiful pea-green boat.*
> *They took some honey, and plenty of money,*
> *Wrapped up in a five-pound note.*

The fraught early days of separation require rather more preparation than this. You will find that your emotions will be running so high, your mood swings so out of control, that the more preparations you can make beforehand the better. What's more, how you behave in these early days may well colour the rest of the story and will certainly have a bearing on how quickly or not you recover.

To start with, as far as you can, don't be rash. I'm assuming that the decision is irreversible and that most people reading this particular chapter are on the receiving end. By rash, I mean don't do anything irrevocable. Don't do anything you cannot undo. For example, you may rightly be in considerable anguish at being forced out of your home. But to damage that home before you are compelled to leave will gain you nothing. To abuse your unfaithful partner in front of the children won't help you. To strike your drunken partner won't help you. Difficult though circumstances are, try not to make matters worse. You are more likely to follow this advice if you have made some preparations beforehand and, even then, you will be surprised at your own behaviour and reactions.

Practical considerations

By now, I assume you will have obtained some professional advice and will not take any important steps without it. Such questions as, 'Where am I going to live?', 'What am I going to live on?' and 'What is to be done with the children?' should be worked out well in advance.

If you are fleeing the family home because life is so intolerable or if you are being pushed out of your home, you must have alternative accommodation available. What is more, such accommodation must be reasonable for your needs and you really cannot expect either your friends or family to have you indefinitely. In an emergency the local authority will help you but the accommodation provided is pretty poor, to say the least. At this difficult time, both you and your children need as much stability as you can get. It is often a great assistance to have accommodation on standby and available for a few months. During those few months, more permanent plans can be made.

As for income, your ability to earn or your partner's ability or willingness to pay, and often both, can go into a sharp decline. The most surprising people have found themselves having to live on state benefits while these problems are resolved. It may be very difficult but if you are likely to end up on your own, it is as well to try and build up some ability to earn before the actual break comes. Very often, if you are a deserted woman with dependent children your skills are rusty and your availability very limited but any efforts you can make to help yourself are worth doing, both for practical reasons and for your own morale, your self-esteem.

As for the children, as stressed again and again, they are the priority. Whatever your own pain in these early days, they must be considered. It is very damaging to take them, without warning, away from the only home, area and school they know. In rare emergencies, this may be necessary. If you are putting them first, you may well have to postpone certain plans until contingency arrangements are in hand. The more links you can keep unbroken the better. In other words, if you have to move away from home, it is better to stay in the same area, at least for a while, so that the children will still be able to see their friends, go to the same school and (whatever your feelings) probably see the other parent. Children dislike change, as Julia Tugendhat's invaluable book, *What Teenagers Can Tell Us About Divorce And Step-Families*, makes very clear.

Helpers

At crisis time, as helpers, we should be the same, letting our friends know that, for a while at least, whatever the time of day and night, they have only to call and we will come. In fact, such offers are rarely taken up, thank goodness, but the very offer is of immense comfort to the person concerned. So, looking them straight in the eyes, tell them, 'Here we are – here's our phone number – just call or phone whenever you feel the need.'

My mother, when nearly 90, said how reassuring it was to know that two doors away were a couple who would be round in a moment should she ever be in trouble. With our friends, we must give them the same reassurance, always remembering that once the first crisis is past their demands are likely to lessen. In addition to this general reassurance, in these early stages practical help, often humble practical help, is valuable. It may well be that offering to do the school run both ways or to bring supper round tonight or take the car to the garage is what they need at this time.

SEVEN

How Can I Help Myself?

Chapter 4 concentrated on the cost of separation: not just the financial cost, though this may be considerable, but the emotional cost – all the pain, guilt, anger, loneliness, which separation entails. This affects not only yourself but your family and friends and, above all, the main victims, the children. Faced with this grim catalogue, enough to depress the most stout-hearted, you may well ask, 'How can I help myself?' A very fair question. Mercifully, there is much you can do. As an American friend once put it, 'You can go through it or you can grow through it.' It may not seem so at the time, but failure can teach you. If you accept the pain and work out and evaluate what the failure means, you can convert it into one of the best, one of the most useful experiences in your life. Easier said than done.

Love yourself

Learn to love yourself. You may never have loved yourself before. Many people don't. Or you may have to rebuild your self-esteem. Either way it is a slow process but infinitely worth undertaking. Start now. Learn to love yourself.

So, love yourself. We are not endorsing pride or conceit, which almost always end in tears. Think of silly, selfish Toad in *The Wind In The Willows* and how often he ended up in trouble! We are talking here of fostering a feeling of self-value, self-esteem, self-worth. Your partner may have reduced you to pulp but your family, your friends, value you. Therefore, step by step, inch by inch, you must rebuild your confidence. Of course outsiders and time can help this process but in the end it is down to you. In human terms, as Rudyard Kipling says, 'The race is run by one and one.' So, brick by brick, rebuild yourself rather differently, perhaps even better than you were before. After all, you will be both older and wiser. Taking the building analogy a little further, please remember the doors and windows as well. In other words let light into your building. There is no point in building a closed self-righteous bitter cell, imprisoning yourself within it. Don't be too hard on yourself.

In a way, it all comes down to attitude. David Helfgott, the Australian pianist, was brilliantly portrayed by Geoffrey Rush in the film *Shine*. Although a brilliant musician, he had a terrible childhood with a monstrous father and ended up in a mental hospital, after a severe nervous breakdown. Years later, he married Gillian who, with consummate love and care, has brought him back to the outside world and back to the concert platform. David Helfgott said, 'We can just be aware of the now. We can cheer up! We can sort of jolly holly our way, can't we?' We can sort of jolly holly our way – yes, we can, but it is mainly down to us.

Blame

At this difficult time, you may be helped and encouraged by a passage from James Dobson which I have successfully quoted at various recovery seminars. It goes as follows:

The blame for marital disintegration is seldom the fault of the husband or wife alone. It takes two to tangle, as they say, and there is always some measure of shared blame for a divorce. However, when one marriage partner makes up his mind to behave irresponsibly, to become involved extramaritally, or to run from his family commitments and obligations, he usually seeks to justify his behaviour by magnifying the failures of his spouse. 'You didn't meet my needs, so I had to satisfy them somewhere else' is the familiar accusation. By increasing the guilt of his partner in this way, he reduces his own culpability. For a husband or wife with low self-esteem, these charges and recriminations are accepted as fact when hurled his way. 'Yes it was my fault. I drove you to it.' Thus the victim assumes the full responsibility for his partner's irresponsibility, and self-worth shatters. (*Doctor Dobson Answers Your Questions*, Kingsway Publications, 1983)

Dr Dobson goes on to encourage you to examine the facts carefully and objectively. Try to answer these questions now although you may well find that you can answer them fairly only after a decent lapse of time.

1 Despite my human frailties, did I value my relationship and try to preserve it?
2 Did my partner decide to destroy it and then seek justification?
3 Was I given a fair chance to resolve the areas of greatest irritation?
4 Could I have held my partner even if I had made all the changes wanted?

Dr Dobson wisely adds,

You should know that social rejection breeds feelings of inferiority and self-pity in enormous proportions. And rejection by the one you love, particularly, is the most powerful destroyer of self-esteem in the entire realm of human experience. You might begin to see yourself as a victim in this process, rather than a worthless failure at the game of love.

On a personal note, if I had had these four questions pinned to my shaving-mirror when I was in distress and had answered them truthfully, I would have recovered my balance and my happiness far sooner. The victims nearly always take upon themselves the guilt of the guilty – so put it back where it belongs.

A grief situation

Appreciate that you are grieving. At the time, I did not consciously realize this. If I had, I am sure that I would have recovered more quickly. Consider somebody recently widowed after years of happy marriage and that it takes months, even years, to 'recover' from the death. You are in the same position but with two additional handicaps. To start with, your memories of your partner are not sanctified by death, they are tainted by divorce. Second, society will rally round the widowed, at least for a while. You will receive little or no such support. I will always contrast the overwhelming support I received over the death of my son Joshua in 1996 with the limited support I received when my marriage went on the rocks in 1980 even though the break-up was more painful.

Furthermore, our Western society does not handle grief wisely, although this is improving. Particularly if we are men we are taught to hide our grief and to put on a bold face, the proverbial stiff upper lip. To a limited extent this may have its uses. Generations differ, as the reactions to the death of Diana, Princess of Wales have shown. We must express our grief and pain in our own way. We must be prepared to work through it. We must weep and be angry, even rant and rave – for a while – and then stop. If we don't work through our own grief, we are only storing up trouble for ourselves later. Illness, depression, even suicide can result from suppressed grief and anger.

A friend, ten years after the death of a child, suddenly exploded in grief for that child. At the time of the death she had been very brave but, internally, had not worked it out. Just as poignantly, I recall another person who lost a child well over twenty years before and had still, even to the casual observer, not recovered.

Again, thinking of the widowed, recall how strangely they can behave with their ups and downs, their good days and their bad. Our situation is similar, without the social support which the widowed rightly get. So, while in this grief situation, be kind to yourself. During mine, I said, did, and thought things which were totally out of character, with violent swings of mood, elation being followed by despair all in the space of a few minutes. It was as if I had lost a protective outer skin, making me hypersensitive – laughter one moment, tears the next.

One friend talked of being 'easily knocked by the small things'. I agree. Perhaps a trivial incident will bring this home. Having just had to leave my wife and children, with another man installed in my place, I was having supper with an elderly cousin who rightly accused me of having taken too much apple tart. To my amazement, I nearly burst into tears. At this time, I was constantly worried that I might burst into tears in court although I never did so. This stage passed. While you are going through this natural and healthy process which leads to healing, try to be objective, saying to yourself, 'This will pass.' After all, following an operation or illness we look after ourselves, we convalesce. Healing takes time. Above all, be patient.

Five years

On the length of time it can take, I don't wish to depress you. However, five years is a useful yardstick, meaning five years from the start of the irrevocable flaw in your relationship to the time, well after you have settled it all, when you can really say, 'It is over. I am okay.' So, if you are reading this book and divorce is under way, you could already be halfway through the five-year period and it is by no means all gloom and doom. Remember, too, the speed of your recovery to health and happiness is partly up to you. Some recover in three years; others don't in a lifetime. You can choose. Avoid too quick a recovery. Likewise avoid too slow a recovery.

Self-pity

Avoid too much introspection. Avoid too much analysis. Appreciate that others have problems; learn and listen to their problems. I certainly didn't follow this advice. As Dobson points out, 'bitterness and resentment are emotional cancers which rot us from within'. Self-pity is a malignant tumour.

Maya Angelou, the bestselling American author, has had an eventful life. She has been a prostitute, a madam, the first black conductor on the San Francisco street cars, a mother at 16, Creole cook, singer, dancer, star of *Porgy and Bess*, civil rights activist with Martin Luther King and is now a poet, university teacher and the highest selling black US female writer. When she was eight, she was raped by her mother's boyfriend.

The man was lynched and beaten to death. For the next five years she didn't or couldn't speak and was repeatedly beaten by her family for 'refusing' to talk. She has this to say about bitterness. 'Bitterness doesn't do a damn thing. It is like a cancer which eats into his host. But anger is like fire' (*Independent*, 23 March 1992).

One cure is to think of others and, believe me, there are always people worse off than you. They desperately need and deserve your help. By helping them, you will help yourself. There is no doubt about this. Time and time again I have seen this come true. Reach out to help others and, almost without your noticing, your own problems become less daunting.

Where to help? The opportunities are endless. Often your own family, neighbours and friends provide a start. A telephone call, a letter, a short visit can produce pleasure out of all proportion to your effort.

Looking more widely, what about local charities if you are very busy, or national charities if you have more time? Locally, there are nine charity shops which are a very good source for books, ties and, occasionally, shirts. All of them need volunteers. Some are temporarily shut for lack of volunteers and, only yesterday, the manageress of the Barnardo's shop told me that she was short of helpers. I am not suggesting a heavy involvement. It is probably not a good idea at this stage but some effort to help others will help you tenfold. Incidentally, choose an enjoyable form of help. If you dislike cooking, don't. If you love sewing, do. Activities which bring you into contact with people are pre-ferable to addressing a thousand envelopes in a lonely bedsitter.

Dame Barbara Cartland has two main claims to fame. She is the step-grandmother of Diana, Princess of Wales and she is the world's most famous romantic novelist. Now in her nineties, she has written over 550 books. I must be one of the few men who have read one, namely *A Virgin in Mayfair* – an unforgettable experience. She is a very active and remarkable old lady and her advice to lonely people is: 'Go to the town hall, ask for a list of charities and join everything. They will all be delighted to have you. When you have made a few friends you can drop the rest.' In many ways, she has got it right.

Hobbies

Consider taking up some hobby or interest which is not demanding or expensive to help break the emotional log-jam. This is very therapeutic; you must be your own physician. Avoid heavy or difficult commitments. Better an evening class in Chinese cooking than starting a five-year course in Mandarin. Better a cycling weekend in France with your brother than joining the Foreign Legion. In other words, get yourself involved in enjoyable lightweight interests which will bring you out of yourself. These hobbies need not be expensive. The library or town hall will undoubtedly help. With some diffidence, I offer a list of possibilities. I have no doubt at all that you can draw up a better list. You could consider aerobics, cooking, cycling, dancing, embroidery, gardening, jogging, knitting, languages, music, museums, painting, reading, swimming, singing or walking.

Of course, parents with little money and young children will find it very difficult to take up any outside interest; survival is difficult enough. All the same, remember what many people have achieved against the odds. Reading recent obituaries, often of people involved in the Second World War, I am humbled by what people have done against almost overwhelming odds. Start reading obituaries and realize how others have suffered and survived.

Laughter

Recently the newspapers mentioned a new remedy for countering stress and despair being pioneered in inner city Birmingham. The treatment costs nothing, has no harmful side-effects, and its applications are virtually limitless. It is called 'laughing'. Doctors have known for many years that laughing reduces muscular tension, improves breathing and regulates the heart beat. It pumps adrenalin into the bloodstream, along with endorphins, the body's chemical painkillers. The contribution of laughter to mental health, although self-evident, has resisted psychologists' attempts to unravel its mechanisms. The old adage about laughter being the best medicine is true. Now you will say, 'How can he write such nonsense? Here am I, with two kids, no partner, no money and no hope and he tells me to laugh – bah!' I can understand this point of view. I would have shared it for a while during my difficulties. However, even if at the moment you cannot solve your problems you can alter your attitude to them. Even in a separation laughter is possible and, quite deliberately, quite consciously, you must try and make room for it.

A few months ago my nine-year-old son Rupert was feeling low because, as a chorister, he had to go back to school. So, the night before his return, off we went to the video shop and hired three videos of *Dad's Army*, the brilliant comedy series about the Home Guard in the Second World War. We lay on duvets in front of the television, eating crisps. He drank lemonade and I drank wine and we laughed and laughed and laughed. My wife said that our laughter could be heard right at the top of the house. It certainly did the trick.

Various suggestions come to mind. One is to surround yourself with wholesome, cheerful, happy people as far as you possibly can. They should not be superficial. The danger is that at a time of crisis, grim vultures circle round and round the dying relationship. You are indeed very vulnerable. Some of these people ('I know what it's like ...', 'I've been through it myself ...', 'They're all the same ...', 'Of course I've always said ...') may mean well. Some don't mean well at all, getting some sick pleasure out of your distress and more practically seeing what pickings are to be had. We all have friends, acquaintances, even family like this. Avoid these people as far as you can. Firmly and politely show them the door. If you are going to retain any buoyancy at all you can't afford to let them drag you down.

Don't only choose happy friends, but also happy events as far as you can. I speak as one who read Thomas Hardy on his honeymoon – not wise! Putting your separation to one side, it is possible to avoid some depressing situations and certainly you can shield your children from them. Better a picnic in the country or in the park than a gloomy film in a dirty cinema. Likewise, with books or films or videos, choose ones which inspire and encourage and entertain, which help to lighten your load.

This leads me to fun. I well recall, in the depths of my divorce, visiting the Portobello Road market in London. The sun shone, the stalls glistened, the crowd swarmed and there was an eccentric old woman pretending to be Vera Lynn holding an old radio in front of her face – and for ten minutes or so, I was completely happy. Quite taken out of myself, just having fun. Poets can do better justice to this mood than I. But the point is that we can quite deliberately place ourselves and our children in situations where fun, laughter, humour are more likely to occur. Do it.

A word of warning. Of course, grief has to be worked through and many practical problems have to be worked out and faced. It is very unwise to stifle either grief or reality. Moreover, humour should not be used artificially like anaesthetic or drink or drugs. It should rather be a pick-up, a boost on a difficult journey. We have all met people who, tragically, never face up to life. I recently saw two very famous comedians on the London Underground. Even allowing for the fact that they were off duty, they had two of the most miserable, even tortured, faces I have ever seen.

Live one day at a time. Agatha Christie, the crime writer, creator of Hercule Poirot, wrote in her autobiography in 1977, 'I like living. I have sometimes been wildly despairing, acutely miserable, racked with sorrow but through it all I still know quite certainly that just to be alive is a grand thing.'

A few years ago, as an observer, I attended a meeting of Alcoholics Anonymous. The evening was very moving, with men and women of differing ages and backgrounds all showing what drink had done to them and how much better they were without it. Their essential message was to take each day at a time. They never said they were cured of alcoholism – they merely said that day, that 24 hours, they had not drunk and they would not drink. Try and adopt their courageous attitude.

The AA prayer is worth memorizing: 'God grant me the serenity to accept the things I cannot change, the courage to change the things I can and the wisdom to know the difference.'

Deep emotional relationships

Don't yet! This is explored later. At the moment, I can only urge you to accept that you are in no fit state to take on any deep relationship. People may say you have only to find someone else and sleep with them for most, if not all, of your problems to disappear. This is just not so. In the short run, the very short run, you may indeed find that your pain is temporarily anaesthetized. Beware. If you continue with the second relationship, there is a very high risk indeed that not only will you make it all the harder honourably to end your first relationship but the jagged edges from your first relationship will seriously harm your second.

Time and time again, we come across people who are in difficulties with their second relationship which are partly, if not over-whelmingly, caused by the unresolved difficulties of their first.

Forgiveness

The central message of this book is forgiveness. If you throw it away and forget all it says, there is no harm done if you remember forgiveness. The clue to recovery is no more and no less than forgiveness. Work through your anger and then start to forgive. This is a continuing process.

The *Daily Mail* on 28 January 1995 said:

> Arm in arm in forgiveness, an Auschwitz victim and a former Nazi doctor walked into the gas chamber. Mozes Kor, 70, chose the 50th anniversary of the camp's liberation to issue a poignant personal amnesty. 'I am relieving myself from pain,' she said. 'It is gone, it is healed. I am letting them off. I am not going to bother with what happened 50 years ago. I can't. I have to get on with my life. I have to let go of that pain. I am doing it more for myself than for them.'

Before the anniversary, she had sought out the SS doctor who had experimented on Jews and had agreed to walk with him back into Auschwitz.

So, attempt to forgive your partner in a small way. Here a little, there a little. For the moment, you are not yet able to forgive the adultery, so how about forgiving the occasional bad temper, the persistent lateness, the refusal to answer important letters and the insistence on leaving the television on, even when friends or family were around. These are minor points but you have to start somewhere.

Finally, and this may take many weeks, even months, start forgiving the major wrongs done to you. Just forgive, thereby releasing not only your partner but also yourself. Like a bird freed from a net, you will be able to fly free again.

EIGHT

How Can Outsiders Help?

Do help all you can. There is no doubt that your help is needed even if it is not appreciated or even acknowledged. The victim is in great pain and wounded animals do tend to bite the hand that feeds them (with the notable exception of Dr Doolittle). They have lost their best friend, their other half, and need your help considerably. It may be needed, with lessening intensity, for a good many years. If you are going to help, you should see the problem through to the end, not the bitter end but the happy end.

An American friend once gently chided us, 'Beware of spreading yourself too thinly.' This always reminds me of strawberry jam. Spread it too thinly and it just doesn't taste! Better to help a few well than many inadequately. This is a problem because life does not bring people to you in neat intervals. They always seem to turn up at the wrong moment. All I can suggest is that while you should never turn down an immediate cry for help, it is as well to have a discreet filter system on hand, so that you can refer the person to somebody else. It is always very rewarding when you are able to refer people for help to those who only a short while ago were themselves in trouble. They often make fine helpers.

Listening

So the need for help is obvious, but how best to do this? Initially this usually involves listening and listening and listening. Often, to endless repetition, inaccuracies and distortions, sometimes even to obscenities. But you must just listen at this stage. For some people you may find that they require intense listening in a formal atmosphere, i.e. the study door closed, you behind your desk, them in front of your desk. With others, this format would not work and they may well only unburden themselves if you go for a walk with the dog or do the washing up together.

Some people like to see you face to face. Some don't. Some find it easier to begin by letter or on the telephone although, in the end, direct contact is usually the best. It is essential to be as approachable as possible. You may even have to initiate the conversation, on the lines of 'You are looking awfully tired' or 'I am sorry that David/Daphne can't come to lunch tomorrow.'

Some of us are better listeners than others. As a lawyer I dislike repetitions, distortions and inaccuracies. My whole training is precision. I know that 'they met in Singapore', why tell me again and again? I know that 'he was made bankrupt in 1982' – why tell me again and again?

Three points may help. First, remember that by merely listening, you are fulfilling a therapeutic purpose. They are being helped towards healing by getting it off their chests, a little like lancing a boil. Second, you can learn a good deal about the situation by noting what they do stress and what they don't. In other words, if Singapore and bankruptcy are important to her then they are important to you. Try and pick up the emotional picture. You can always get the factual picture later, either from the victim, when calmer, or from elsewhere. Third, if you are not a good listener, you can enable others to listen. Thus, on occasions, I'll relieve my wife Caroline by taking the children out for a walk or giving them a bath so that she can listen in peace. She is much better at this. Afterwards, if the other person agrees, we can then discuss it together.

Sometimes, the person is quite unable to say what they are feeling. They may turn up out of the blue, giving a silly excuse, hanging around, looking miserable. It may be tempting to get rid of them but, if you can summon the patience, try to give them space and time and privacy so that they can tell you what is on their mind. Sometimes, you will have to wait. At other times, a direct approach may be needed. 'Look, Fred, are you really worried sick about ...?'

Confidentiality

This leads to confidentiality. Confidentiality is vital. The person must feel that secrets will be kept secret. Even if some of them are little secrets, if told in confidence they must remain in confidence. This is easier said than done particularly with 'minor' confidences. You probably wouldn't tell the world that someone had been abused as a child but you might well let slip that they ate six Mars bars a day. Both are breaches of trust. Indeed, in some situations, they might be as hurt by the one disclosure as the other. So take confidentiality seriously.

Sometimes, of course, you want to discuss this matter with other people. If so, always ask the person if this is alright with them. Usually, if they trust you and know why you want a second opinion, they will agree but you must ask first.

An urgent plea to the older generation

Some of us, blessed with growing families and responsible jobs, don't have so much time to listen. Once we know the facts we can help swiftly and practically but our time and energies are limited. Nearly every day I get up at 6.45 a.m. and go to bed at midnight. It is a constant battle to fit everything and everyone in and I often fail to do so. On the other hand, some retired people have a lot of time on their hands and they can be involved. They have the time and they have the wisdom. Our remaining three parents have just under 250 years' life experience between them. They have seen and done it all. Death, divorce, disaster, wars and wills – an endless source of advice, wisdom and loving support. Not enough of us tap in to the older generation.

Both my wife and I are in constant touch with our own parents. Their experience and advice is invaluable even if, at times, we don't always follow it!

Acceptance

If you listen you must accept people as they are. By this, I don't mean that you should condone or encourage the bad behaviour, but you should always love the person. So when listening to whatever filth comes out, always try to get them to realize that you love them. The very confession brings it into the open and into the light, so in one sense its evil effect has diminished even if there is still work to be done. So don't interrupt. Give them the space and the time. Don't condemn. Don't be judgemental.

This acceptance can be very difficult. Whereas some sins such as mild violence, drinking, even adultery, may well be within our range of experience (either personal or general) others are not. Except in a professional capacity, I have never met anyone who has committed incest or murder. If told, what would I do? I frankly don't know.

This leads to a further important point. Be discerning. If the problem is too big for you to handle (and some problems are) then, firmly but lovingly, you must decline to handle it. If you don't decline, you will not help the victim and you could well hurt yourself. In these rare instances, I would suggest saying the following, 'John/Jane, thank you for telling me. I still love/like you but I can't handle this alone. Let's go and see X and I will stay with you for as long as you need me. I won't let you and the family down. I am sure X can help.' What is more, you should not only follow up this promise but, in normal social ways, you should keep up with them, otherwise they will think they have been dropped because of what they told you.

Only a few weeks ago, in a different context, I encountered this problem head on. A friend arrived out of the blue who was obviously mentally ill. I had just come home from work and my wife and children were milling around waiting for tea. He had recently been released from a mental hospital and, clearly to my lay eyes, the sooner he got back there the better. What could I do? Fighting back a mounting feeling of helplessness, I resolved that, come what may, I would stand by him until I got him back into the safety of hospital. It took over five hours to do so – red tape galore – but it worked and, by 10 p.m., I was home and he was safe. I didn't attempt to help beyond that because I just didn't know what to do. Let the professionals handle it as, indeed, in this case they did to a happy conclusion.

Encouragement

Throughout our helping, we should always try to encourage. Our friends' self-esteem has been shattered, their lives are in ruins. We should always try to encourage them, helping them to rebuild their lives and the lives of their children. Such encouragement should never be superficial or silly. Hope must be based on reality. It is not honest or kind to say that 'he'll give up drinking' or 'she'll come back' when they won't. All the same you can stand by them in their hour of need, gently, quietly suggesting that there is light and life at the end of the tunnel. You can help them rebuild their own dignity.

Normally, we are only called upon to help the 'victim', the so-called 'innocent party'. In my experience the 'guilty' party tends to avoid, like the plague, any friend or relation who might try to dissuade them from breaking up the relationship. They will run the proverbial mile rather than face anyone who may tell them to behave honourably. All the same, they have their problems even if they richly deserve some of them, and we should love and encourage them without in any way condoning or encouraging their bad behaviour. This distinction is sometimes fine but essentially we must continue to love them. Although they may not know it now their behaviour may well end in disaster, even if years later.

It is so easy to be judgemental. Indeed, I only have to read the newspaper to find condemnation rising in my gorge. 'How can he do that?' 'How can she do this?' – and the breakfast table quivers!

Some years ago, a friend whom I liked and admired behaved very badly to his wife. For six months, I was so angry that I felt quite unable to speak to him at all except when I had to. However, I eventually realized that this attitude was 'holier than thou' and not helping at all. I began to see him again. He was not reconciled to his wife and our friendship is not as it was before, yet it still has some value.

The point is, we must not be judgemental.

Furthermore, in some cases the more you know the parties concerned, the harder it becomes to discover the truth, or at least, the rights and wrongs.

Seeing both sides

Often in helping, we see only one of the couple. I well recall drafting a divorce petition in my chambers and being unusually appalled at the conduct of the husband towards his wife. Yet some months later, meeting the wife in court, I could understand what drove him to it. I was almost amazed at his moderation. Alternatively, later events may well justify reinterpreting earlier events. Thus, if you find that not only the first but the second and the third partner leave on the grounds of unreasonable behaviour, you may be driven to the conclusion that, despite outward charm, the person concerned is a little difficult to live with.

Be practical. When you have caught your finger in the door or have dropped a hammer on your toe can you think straight? General Booth, the founder of the Salvation Army, in the last century, put it very well: 'No one gets a blessing if they have cold feet and nobody ever got saved while they had toothache!' Those in the middle of a separation are in pain and, very often, their practical needs demand immediate attention. Once these have been solved or at least lessened, then you can help them emotionally, but first things first. When I was going through a very rough time, it was the cup of soup in the kitchen, the sympathetic ear, that brought me through rather than open emotional support.

Money

Let's be blunt and talk money. One of the tragedies of separation is that the cake cannot be cut into two cakes of similar size. Even the rich find out that their funds are not unlimited. The poor are hit all the harder and, so often, the weak go to the wall. We may well have to help financially and the main problem here is not so much appreciating this as finding ways to make our assistance palatable. People don't like charity. For the moment, I can only suggest that even small sums of money, whether anonymous or not, can work wonders, just like yeast. We are only trustees of our money. Let us use it as generously as we can.

I am not advocating white lies because we should always strive to tell the truth, but if we can sugar the pill of our charity so much the better. Some minor examples spring quickly to mind – an aunt who sent £100 to her five nephews and nieces because an insurance policy had suddenly matured; a friend who arrived with seven bottles of wine, saying they were left over from a party; a friend arriving with an enormous casserole saying, 'Well, since I was making one, it seemed silly not to make another for you at the same time.'

Hospitality

Be inclusive. A woman friend of ours, deserted with three young children, recently wrote: 'I really value my friends who still include me in things, because although I am not a couple I have more in common with married friends with children than single friends who tend to have no commitments so more time and money to play with.'

Include them socially. Separation is cruel in the way that it disrupts most social relationships and often those going through it suffer particularly badly. Their friends or acquaintances do not know where they stand or what to do, with the result that they are dropped altogether. So, try to include them in parties and picnics and the like, even if they are a little depressing and even if they usually refuse. Ask them all the same. The invitation matters. The old and widowed are likewise often ignored. Only the other day, an old lady said: 'I like to be asked. I wouldn't have gone but I like to be asked.' Women suffer far more badly in this area than men.

Don't match-make! It is neither kind nor sensible to put additional pressure on people at this stage. Moreover, it usually doesn't work. The 'couple syndrome' has a good deal to answer for. When you were single, you often attended parties where the sexes were not evenly balanced. Once you are a pair, there is an increasing pressure to be neat and tidy socially. Man, woman, man, woman, man, woman, neatly round the supper table, with, perhaps, two single people for whom you have hopes. We can surely do better than this.

Invite single people to your home, and don't worry if the numbers aren't right. This is particularly supportive to those going through a separation because many people, both male and female, submerge their individual personalities when they are together, increasingly lacking independent identity. They are less well equipped to cope on their own than the single people who have had to paddle their own canoe for many years.

Then try to get them involved outside themselves by making gentle challenges. Often they are so wrapped up with their own problems (which may well be very difficult) that they just can't lift their heads up at all to look beyond the grim present to the possible future. You can help by making small challenges. 'Could you possibly give us an hour at the school fête?' ... 'Could you possibly help at the school sports day?' ... these suggestions are not demanding. They are mild challenges and are intended to help the person build up damaged self-esteem. You should try to strike a balance between imposing on them and treating them as invalids. Consider those who care for the old, the invalid or the handicapped. If they do their job well, they never undermine their charges' dignity, always helping them to do their best, at the same time being there in case they fail or fall.

Time

Also don't forget time. With your own partner's consent, you may have to spend some time helping them. Who is going to mow the lawn? Who is going to collect Granny from the station now that the car has got to be sold? Who is going to help Jane through puberty now that Mum is in Australia as Dad has always been inordinately shy? The opportunities are endless. With just a little thought and a little time, five minutes here or five minutes there, great assistance can be given. Using your imagination, put yourself in their shoes. How are they going to cope? Specific help is often far more valuable than mere general benevolence.

In life's rough passages, I am more than ever convinced that small acts of kindness have a value out of all proportion to what is actually done or said. It is not too melodramatic to point out that potential suicides have changed their minds because of some small act of concern, sometimes from a complete stranger.

To summarize: we should love those in trouble and should not be afraid to show our love practically.

NINE

What About the Children?

Polly Toynbee, writing in the *Independent* newspaper, says it all: 'The research pours out showing that the children of divorce tend to do badly in terms of health, education, and happiness. The effects last into later life and they are more likely to suffer depression, commit suicide, die in accidents, drink heavily, take worse jobs than their peers and get divorced.' My files are brimming with such statements and I am sure that they are right.

Visit any criminal court in the land on any day of the week and you will see how true this is. Even though the social enquiry reports are not read out publicly, time and time again it is quite clear to all that the person in the dock is partly there because of a faulty start in life. A typical court report would read:

Joe Smith was born in London in 1980. Shortly after his birth, his parents separated for ten months until they became reconciled for two stormy years until 1982, when his sister (now adopted) was born. In 1986 when he was six, after witnessing several serious acts of violence between his parents, he was taken to live with his grandmother. This proved successful until she died in 1992, three days before his twelfth birthday. By then his mother, now an alcoholic, had moved away and his father was nowhere to be found ...

Is it any wonder that the child concerned found it hard to grow up a decent citizen?

Mercifully, many do. Furthermore, although much modern thinking is against this, we are all responsible for our actions. It is not good enough to put all the blame on our parents or lack of parents. These factors should be taken into consideration but, if we are to have any human dignity at all, we must be responsible for our own actions.

We should never forget that when people separate, children can be deprived and neglected although materially rich. Separation is no respecter of social background. Its effects are less immediately apparent when the parents are comfortably off but they are just as real to the 'poor little rich girl' or 'poor little rich boy'.

Children first

Faced with these facts, any parent should feel very concerned about separation. But this book will have no purpose at all if it does not attempt to help and encourage those facing such problems. Frankly it will be a damage limitation exercise; some damage is inevitable but we can limit it – we must limit it. Let's go back to the house picture. The house has to be destroyed, much though we dislike the idea. Do we want to dismantle it with some care or do we want to demolish it angrily, with ball and chain, so that beams and bricks will fall on the heads of the children and dust choke them? A crude picture perhaps, but worth bearing in mind.

So, now that separation has begun, what can we do as parents and helpers? The answer is a good deal.

How can the parents help?

Underlying all, we must remember that the children are the priority. Their welfare is the most important thing. Now, by saying this, I am not suggesting that they should be the centre of attention, the heroes of a sordid drama, with all eyes upon them. I would advocate the opposite. Far too many parents tell their children far too much. It may give the parents temporary relief but it can do the children permanent harm.

None the less, quietly and lovingly, they should be considered all the time. Logically, this means that if their interests were truly considered, the parents wouldn't separate at all. By continuing their behaviour, they have firmly put their interests before those of the children. Ironically, parents are most needed when they are least able to help because of their own difficulties – and the children may well be particularly demanding. But, realistically, I'll assume that separation is inevitable and we will all have to do the best we can under the circumstances.

Telling them straight

The aim of both parties, whatever their conduct and whatever their feelings towards each other, should be that the children should have a good relationship throughout their lives with both parents. Therefore, even if Mum has committed adultery and put her own pleasure before her duty as wife and mother, or even if Dad has continually drunk to excess, well knowing that this would ruin the relationship, she is still the children's mother and he is still the children's father. Furthermore, except in rare circumstances, she is still the best mother for the child and he is still the best father. There are exceptions, but generally an imperfect mother is better for a child than a perfect foster mother. Without wishing to attack the social welfare authorities (who face enormous problems, with very difficult cases and very little funds), I must say it is very sad indeed when children are not brought up in a family atmosphere, preferably their own.

In December 1992, the Jubilee Policy Group, based in Cambridge, published *Relational Justice, A New Approach to Penal Reform*. With Home Office approval, 358 prisoners in 20 prisons were interviewed in the summer of 1992; of the 330 men, 29 per cent had been in care as children.

So parents, whatever their feelings towards each other, should try to have their children living with one or other of them and should try to assist their children to have a good relationship with both. This can be particularly hard on a parent where the other parent is behaving badly. I don't know the complete answer but I suggest that, without condoning the conduct of the other parent, we can honestly say 'Well, I know that Dad's difficult when he has had too much to drink but he is your dad. He loves you very much and you must try to do what he says – when he is sober.'

Early on, in order to lay the foundations of a good relationship, ideally both parents should tell the children the truth – commensurate with their ability to understand. Explain as best you can and answer any questions as they come up.

This is difficult, very difficult and it is particularly hard for the guilty party but, if they have any decency left, they should try. The younger the children, the vaguer the account. You shouldn't lie but there is no point in telling them the unsavoury details. Better to say, 'My loves, you know Mummy and I haven't been happy for a long time. Well, we are going to live in different houses. Mummy is going to look after you and I am going to see you every weekend and we will have fun.'

These words sound hollow and trite; indeed, they are, because in a real sense the children have been betrayed by their parents. But it's the best you can do. As the children get older, or if they are older already, you can fill in the details but no more than is necessary. There is no point in getting at the other party under the pretext of 'telling the children the truth'. Never use the children as weapons to 'get at your partner'. Incidentally, the truth will out anyway. If you are 'innocent', you don't have to justify yourself. If you are 'guilty', you can't justify yourself. Let time and truth provide the answer gradually.

Dr Robin Skynner is a most experienced psychiatrist who, together with John Cleese, wrote a fascinating book on *Families and How to Survive Them*. Writing some years ago in the *Radio Times*, he said: 'Many people believe that it is harmful for parents to reveal their feelings to their children, but family interviews have long convinced me that children can handle almost any kind of disclosure as long as it is the truth.' This truth, even if diluted, should come from the parents. As it is, many children learn that their parents are separating from a third party. Parents often do not talk to their children and ask them what they want or, at the very least, tell them what is going to happen.

In my own case, when I had to leave my home when my daughter was eight, I gave her no explanation why, thinking that the answer was obvious. It was, to my adult eyes, but to her it wasn't and, for many years, she considered that I had walked out. If only I had faced the music then, a good deal of pain could have been avoided.

Whether you decide to tell the children alone or together, try to be as objective and fair as possible. How you do so is entirely up to you but I was recently given some tips which I will happily pass on. They are as follows:

1 Decide in advance how you are going to explain it to the children and ensure that both of you are present when they are told. Don't let them hear two different versions.

2 Be as frank as is reasonably possible. Don't try to bluff them by giving implausible scenarios or by suggesting the separation is temporary when you know it is not.

3 Assure them that they are loved as much as ever and that they are not to blame in any way. Emphasize this strongly ... 'It's not your fault.'

4 Emphasize the things that will not change in their lives. Children are conservative and find the thought of upheaval stressful.

5 It is not necessary to pretend to be the best of friends when you are not. But try at least to be cordial to each other in the presence of the children.

6 Work hard at making arrangements of visits and handovers in advance. Don't humiliate your children.

Don't despair. Separation can be an opportunity for parents to improve their relationships with their children. I cannot thank the writer of this advice because I do not know who he or she is. But I have to say I endorse every word.

About this time, preferably together or, at the very least, by a joint letter, the children's schools should be told. So often, in this unhappy time, the school is a port in the storm. What's more, it's only fair on the school teachers to warn them, because your children's behaviour and performance may well go downhill at this time.

Parental role

Lord Donaldson, the former Master of the Rolls, said in 1992, 'Good parenting involves giving minors as much rope as they can handle without an unacceptable risk that they will hang themselves.' He couldn't have put it better.

Your next ambition should be to remain a parent, not a pal,

to your children and to help the other parent retain some parental dignity. Don't let the children manipulate. Children are most secure, happy and relaxed when they know an adult is firmly in control.

We must remain parents, and in a sense we must keep our distance and help the other parent to do the same. Now, I am not suggesting the Victorian image of papa seen for half an hour after tea. I am all for bathing the children, changing the nappies, cutting the grass and so on. All the same, we are parents. We should never forget it. The breakdown of parental responsibility, the way in which many parents have opted out of their respon-sibilities, is one of the main causes of society's problems today. Such parents are equipping their children very badly for later life.

So as parents, we must not spoil our children. We didn't when we were living with them and we shouldn't when we are apart from them. Naturally, if we only see them once a week, we will give them a better tea. But don't overdo it. Those who attempt to buy the children's love by spoiling them are doing the children great harm even if, temporarily at least, it appears to work. It is emotional blackmail and as a wise old High Court judge once told me, blackmail is sometimes worse than murder.

If the other parent is trying to buy the children's affection away from you – and this happens all too often – what can you do? Sometimes very little. But, in my experience, if you love them and understand them they will usually stick by you, particularly if you remember to make life enjoyable. Helping them make a cake and then ice it, followed by a borrowed video of *Tom and Jerry*, can work wonders. Children are often far shrewder and more loyal than we realize. In short, your influence over and your effect upon the children is much more dependent on your loving relationship with them than on the time and money you spend on them. Mind you, this is always provided that you aren't spending all your time and money on horses and drink!

Don't make it difficult

Access (the new in-word is 'contact' but it means access) is as easy or as difficult as you, the parents, make it. Thousands of parents handle it with care and common sense, oiled by humour. The problems are minimal. On the other hand, a few parents make it as difficult and nasty as they possibly can. You can see more unpleasantness, more naked hate in custody/ contact disputes than on many a battlefield. It is a battlefield, the parents working out their bitter hatred of each other, using the children as pawns, inflicting incalculable damage upon them. Beware of getting into such a situation because it can escalate out of all proportion. Sometimes only one party is really to blame, but it often takes two. The more reasonable we are to our former partner the more chance there is of establishing a working relationship over the children. So the sooner you start to forgive and forget the better, even during the trauma of the actual separation.

Flexibility should be your aim. You were flexible when you were happily married. Why not be flexible now that you are not? In other words, don't be too rigid. If she wants to alter that weekend because her cousin has suddenly come over from Australia, agree. If he wants to take your son to a football match because a spare ticket is suddenly available, let him. And so what if, from time to time, the children come home a little late or a little dirty? Certain parents, sometimes encouraged by their solicitors, fight over the most trivial of details. They are inflicted with '10 minute late syndrome'. Please don't be. If one parent lives in east London and the other parent lives in west London and there is a football match or a march on Saturday afternoon, is it really all that surprising if the children are delivered a little late? Of course it isn't. Tolerance can be abused and limits may have to be set but, generally, an easy to and fro is much better than rigid guidelines. The older the children, the more the flexibility.

The right of contact

Two important points are worth noting here. First, if at all possible, try to live close by. I am eternally grateful to my two older children, then aged ten and eight, for asking me to move back to Chiswick, where they lived with their mother in my former home, when I had moved to Fulham intending to remain there. As they put it, 'It will be much easier for us, Daddy.' Although painful at the time, in the end it has been well worth doing. In some instances, this cannot be done and some parents who have the custody of the children have deliberately moved, sometimes abroad, in order to thwart the relationship with the other parent. Generally, you can live close by, even if it means rejecting that good job offer.

Second, and I well remember the pain, try and keep up contact however hard it is for you. After all, seeing your children in your home with the lover in your dressing-gown at your table with your wife is pain indeed. But the pain will pass and the children need you. Access is *their right*, not yours. As Lord Justice Elizabeth Butler-Sloss, who chaired the Cleveland enquiry, has said, 'It is the children's right, not the right of the parent, to have a continuing relationship with the non-custodial parent.' This requires courage. I have never forgotten an admirable man, so distressed by his wife's adultery that he refused ever again to see their two sons because of the pain it caused him. This may be quite understandable but the sons needed him and he was a good man in a responsible position with much to offer them. The moral is: persevere.

Incidentally, during or after contact visits, never pump the children for information about the other parent. 'I see that Mum's got a new car.' 'Did you like Dad's new girlfriend?' It is not right. However subtly done, the children will see through your questions and be hurt by them. How much should they tell you? Are they being disloyal to Dad? Didn't Mum say not to tell about Arthur? The children will tell you what they want to tell you. It is not fair to probe. What is more, your job is to build up your own self-esteem. You won't do this by looking over your shoulder at the past. Concentrate on your present and your future and that of your children. For years I didn't follow this advice, thereby hurting myself and confusing my children.

Finally, stress that the separation is not their fault. Apparently many children feel that their parents broke up because they were 'naughty' or 'expensive' or whatever. All children need the reassurance that they are not to blame. It is terrible to think that they should have to carry this burden when they have burdens enough anyway. They may well not say this, knowing that it would hurt and anger you. You may have to get them to talk about the way they feel, possibly to a close friend or a wise grandparent or godparent. It is the thorn which must be pulled out as quickly and painlessly as possible.

Two final points: firstly, it has been wisely said that a parent's influence is much more dependent upon the relationship that parent has with the children than upon the amount of time spent with them. If you have a good relationship with your children and they know that you are utterly and completely 'with them' when you are with them then all will go well. On the other hand, if you only have six hours with them and spend four in a pub with your own friends or three asleep in front of the television, then they will very soon get bored and restless. It is essential that you plan your time with them almost like a military operation. Don't overdo it but don't underdo it.

Secondly, and this point has probably caused more court cases than any other, the fact that one parent may have been extremely nasty to the other does not necessarily mean that they are not devoted parents to their children, with the children loving them very much and missing them like mad. He may have beaten you around, she may have been disgustingly drunk, but children, thank goodness, nearly always love us whatever our faults.

How can the helper help?

One in five families with dependent children are headed by a lone parent. They need help.

One of the duties of the advocate, solicitor or barrister, is to assimilate the facts and law of a case and feed them in palatable form to the judge and, sometimes, the jury. 'All judges are perfect but some are more perfect than others.' Thus, if you have a quick-witted judge your submission can be pithy. Alternatively, if you have an old stickler (and there are still a few), you will have to adjust your submissions accordingly. It is a case of horses for courses.

The helper faced with the victim should do the same. Nothing will be gained by being dominant or bossy. The parent is vulnerable, so are the children, and it is all too easy for those of us who are not emotionally involved to offer advice. By all means do, but cautiously and lovingly or not at all. You may find it useful to listen to various tapes and read various books, perhaps making some notes of your own. Once you have fully digested the contents, then and only then can you gently spoon-feed them to those who need help. My father-in-law is masterly at this. Drawing on his pipe, he'll begin by saying, 'We were just wondering ...' or 'I have been thinking over that problem ...' Wise, pertinent advice then follows, but so graciously that we listen and usually follow it.

What's more, many people faced with a relationship in trouble among their friends just cannot cope at all. They should cope but they can't cope. If so, and if you cannot face either of the parents, could you not at least consider the children and face them? They are innocent and they do need you.

Your own children can help too

What is more, your own children can help too. It is good for children to appreciate their own good fortune and that we should, all of us, young or old, lovingly serve one another. Your four-year-old can have a child to tea. Our young children did so recently when a young mother died of cancer. Harriet, when seven, inspired by the children's TV programme *Blue Peter*, ran a bring-and-buy sale for the blind people in Africa and raised £300. Your fourteen-year-old can be asked, or even told, to take someone on a bike ride or for a swim.

There was recently a fascinating programme on television about a small state school in Wales. Faced with an increasing number of children whose parents were not living together, the headmaster decided not to get the parents to help but, with the parents' permission, to involve the children. Some of those children were interviewed and their remarks were very moving. Time and time again they said that they didn't mind discussing their problems with their friends (who had been through the same thing and were usually a little older) because their friends 'understood'. Their message was that they didn't want to discuss these matters with their parents or with the teachers – one, because they were grown up and two, they just wouldn't understand. This experiment obviously requires careful handling but is well worth bearing in mind. Leading from this, don't ignore young cousins if you have them. My wife and I both have numerous cousins whose friendship and contact can wax and wane but has been a constant thread throughout our lives.

Include the children on treats but make the treats as normal and natural as possible. Don't patronize, don't overwhelm. The victim parent is very vulnerable and very sensitive. They don't want charity but they do need help, particularly for their children. So why not invite the child to join you for a day at the seaside (which incidentally gives Mum a break) or your visit to the local cinema with supper afterwards? Be inclusive. Informal treats are probably the best of all.

Standing in

A letter by a Mr Bradford on 8 April 1997 in *The Times* put it well: 'Sir, the female orgasm pill, even if it were to be combined with paracetamol to prevent headaches, is all very well but it still won't mow the lawn.'

You can stand in for the missing parent. So if you are good at football, why not ask young Tom to join your son in a kickabout? If you are near a deserted father with two young girls, why not ask them round to help make the cakes for the school play? The feminists may dislike these stereotypes but I am unrepentant. The child needs both parents. We can, within limits, be role models.

Some years ago, a friend gave tea to two children whose mother had suddenly died and whose father did not come home each night until about six o'clock. For many months, she calmly and quietly bridged a vulnerable gap. Again, I think of a deserted mother with three young children. The youngest, a boy of about five, was particularly active and live-ly. He had a young godfather, in his early twenties. Week in, week out, this young godfather took on a role somewhere between father and big brother to the immense benefit of the little boy. And, incidentally, to himself now that he has a child of his own.

The role of grandparents

The older generation have much to offer. One of the saddest truths when parents separate is that not only does the child lose, or partly lose, a parent but, so often, the grandparents on the losing side are even more pushed out of the picture. 'Oh, my son and I haven't seen the grandchildren for years ever since the separation.' How often does one hear this? If older, we can help the children. We have the time. Many parents don't. We can remember them on their birthday and at Christmas. We can send them postcards on holiday. We can go to their school functions. It need not cost much but the rewards are high. Indeed, many an old person has benefited enormously.

All this presupposes that the parent welcomes such help. Some do not.

If you know the circumstances, you can sometimes help with money. Expense can be minimal, but it need not be. As we all know, separation is expensive for everyone concerned and very often the parent with the children is struggling to make ends meet on a limited and uncertain budget. Instead of an anonymous donation to a charity, why not consider the problem on your doorstep? Cash may well be embarrassing, so perhaps you can help in kind. Well worth doing. Although you want to help, perhaps in gratitude for your own happy family life or because you yourself have now recovered from an unhappy time, you may not actually know of any particularly deserving cause. Look around or ask. At this very moment, I can think of parents and children who are in deep trouble, practically and emotionally. Wherever you are, people need help. I heard recently of a man who 'had so much money he didn't know what to do with it'. This remark still rankles, considering the difficulties so many people face. Alternatively, if there really are no needy cases in your neighbourhood then a contribution to a national charity is always welcome.

Nearer home, some parents with children to entertain on contact visits have no suitable home to which to take them. Walking around the park in a hailstorm is not much fun. You have a house; why not lend it? Only those of us who have lived with our family in a family house and then lost it can fully understand this. I make no apologies for repeating this point. All your heart and probably all your money and all your possessions, except your toothbrush, are in that house and not only are you effectively banned from it but you may well have the additional pain of knowing that somebody, quite improperly, is living in it. Saturday comes. The children are dropped outside your bedsitter. What are you to do with them? The friend who picks you up and lends his home is a friend indeed. If those friends, having given you all lunch, can then leave you alone with the children until after tea, so much the better.

There are official contact centres. In many ways, they are admirable, filling an undoubted gap, but they are institutional and are often overcrowded, with limited opening hours. A private home is better.

Absent parents

Finally, when you are with the children, it sometimes helps to mention the absent parent, but not critically or obtrusively.

To over-mention is as damaging as to under-mention. But such a phrase as, 'I first met your daddy fishing, do you like fishing?' can help rebuild the damaged image in the child's mind. At home, daddy may not be mentioned at all. Always refer to 'mummy' or 'daddy' or 'mum' or 'dad'; 'your mother' or 'your father' is chillingly formal.

Postscript

Dr Robin Skynner has written the following:

I was reassured by a trip I made to a prestigious girls' school in Dallas, Texas, some years ago. During the visit a number of the pupils described their experience of their parents' divorce. Although very painful, it seemed to have left them more confident and resilient. Fellow pupils with intact families seemed envious and looked more immature than these class mates. Now, I am sure there are better ways of gaining confidence, but I no longer see divorce as quite the unmitigated disaster I once did.

After a Divorce
or Separation

TEN

Tying Up Loose Ends

The decree has been made absolute. You have obtained your divorce. All the separation details have been worked out. You are free. Legally the matter is settled, but emotionally there is still much work to be done. Indeed, in many ways, the decree absolute or separation agreement is irrelevant and it is almost always an anticlimax. The essential point to grasp is that unless yours was a short relationship with no children, in a sense a separation is never final. As I have said before, it is not an event; it is a process.

Whether or not you had children, the longer the relationship, the longer the aftermath. Your families, your friends, even your acquaintances, will be intermingled. Disentangling takes time; the more carefully it is done, the better for your future happiness.

A dignified exit

If you do have children your responsibilities towards them will continue, or at least should continue, until your death. However, these responsibilities do change. When our children have finished their full-time education, we are responsible for them although, naturally, our relationship will alter with the years. Likewise, as we get older, our children may have to be responsible for us. It is a two-way traffic of mutual support and encouragement based on love. The parent/child relationship may well be very damaged by the separation but it shouldn't be severed. Again, how we handle matters now, just after the separation, will affect our relationship with our children and our grandchildren for many years to come.

In short, recovery is a process and your attitude is crucial. There is an instructive tale of two young women who were widowed. One was emotionally crippled as a result of her experiences and spent the rest of her life unhappy and causing unhappiness. She was embittered, only considering herself. The other, having worked through her grief, devoted the rest of her life to loving and helping others. The external facts were similar; their inner reactions totally different.

Quite a useful picture is to envisage athletes running in a race, passing the finishing line yet continuing to run for quite a distance before they walk and ultimately rest altogether. It would harm them if they stopped dead just past the finishing line. Likewise, while we are splitting up, our energies and those of our family and friends have all been geared up to the finishing line. But we should still continue to run for a little while, as should our helpers, because there is still work to be done.

Another analogy may assist. Reverting to the picture of the marriage as a house, the house has now been demolished by divorce. The site has still to be cleared. You can either have an ugly bombsite, with weeds, rubble and craters, which can harm you and others. Or you can level the site, putting down stone or gravel which require minimum maintenance.

Living in London, I pass derelict buildings nearly every day, their walls covered with graffiti, their windows gaping, their gardens a mass of bottles, cans and weeds. These buildings are an eyesore and a danger. If you enter them you could get hurt, even killed. But once the site is landscaped, not only is the danger removed but the whole townscape is improved. These analogies obviously mustn't be taken too far, but I have found them quite useful both for myself and for others.

Don't look back

You can't walk forward looking backwards. The key is to forget the former things. Emotional spring-cleaning is required. You must learn to let go of the past, always remembering that your former partner is no longer your property or your problem. Of course, particularly if you have children, you may have to have some dealings together but you must sever the emotional tie. Not easy; some people never do it. But on the assumption that most of us who are divorced do so before middle age, do remember that we should have another 30 or 40 years of life to live. Far better to live those years in the present, looking to the future, than being trapped in the past, an ever-receding past.

You were a partnership. Now you are not. It is essential you learn to lead an independent life. You must try not to be hurt by the successes or delighted by the failures of your former partner. Few, if any of us, live up to this perfection but, for our own health and happiness, we should certainly try to do so. In short, it's harmful to look back. Splitting up is traumatic, no doubt about it. It is one of life's major milestones but life goes on. If you split up in 1980, in very unhappy circumstances, you may well be in turmoil for some months, even years afterwards. But it is now 1998, with the millennium fast upon us. Unless you move on from 1980, in a very real sense you will be trapped in 1980 and, as time goes on, this will be increasingly sad. Not to let go of your former partner is a form of perverted emotional attachment, with none of the pleasure and all of the pain.

Mothers trapped with children understandably find it particularly hard to move on. It is much easier for those of us who can get out of the home, back into the mainstream of life. Even here, however, as one mother with three young children told me, 'Peace comes from within and I wanted to concentrate on finding peace in myself first.' She used her very limitations of time and money to let go of the past before moving on.

Another picture is of those old-fashioned gramophones where the needle had a tendency to stick in the groove, endlessly repeating itself: '... and then I found the letter in her handbag', 'after that I was in hospital for eight days', '... and he never even remembered Tom's birthday'. Please don't get stuck in these grooves. It is not healthy for you or for others. A friend of mine was a musician, a singer of some merit. I was talking to a group on this topic and used this gramophone example. His face fell and then, to my delight, he stood up and with a laugh said, 'You're talking about me!' I was at that time, but the good news was that, after he had thought it through, he 'pushed the needle on' and quite soon became much happier – and much better company for his family and friends.

To help avoid this it is as well to trim as many loose ends as possible. Some people, whether consciously or not, prolong the aftermath of a divorce, endlessly finding problems which necessitate contact with the other side. Thus, even ten years after a divorce, solicitors may still be investigating the small print of a time-share agreement or the ultimate destination of the piano. If you possibly can, don't do this. Far better to have a clean break, even if this means that you have to concede points rather than protract proceedings. Let her have the piano rather than spend hundreds of pounds over many years haggling over ownership. In short, you should 'clear the decks', always remembering that if you have not sorted out old issues with your parents or your previous partners you are all the more likely to find yourself entrapped in similar conflicts in your new relationships.

The Times in January 1995 had an amusing article on this very topic. One barrister recollected an estranged couple who were fighting over two Kenwood mixers. The woman, apparently, wanted to keep both. Another lawyer recollected a case in which the couple were fighting over 10 loo rolls. The husband was going to America and didn't see why he should go without his loo rolls. But my favourite was a letter written by David Foskett QC on 19 January 1995. He wrote, 'Sir, divorce disputes concerning train sets, Kenwood mixers and even loo rolls are but nothing. I was once involved in a matrimonial case in which a major issue was the final resting place of a stuffed woodpecker.'

On a personal note, my first wife and I had collected enamel advertising signs during our 10 years together and, on separation, I was particularly keen to have one of a black cat advertising Kensitas cigarettes which was on the wall outside our daughter's bedroom. She was then aged eight. When my wife began to unscrew it my daughter became hysterical, begging her not to. She phoned me at once and I immediately said, 'No problem, forget about it. Let's give it to Emily and it must stay on the wall.' It did. A few days later, without prompting, my wife brought round our favourite enamel of all, which was twice as large and showed five little men holding a paint brush. A nice gesture. We were all in the right.

Only a few months ago, while sorting out my desk, I found a letter which could have reopened an issue with my wife from whom I have been divorced for many years. We now get on well. I just threw the letter in the waste-paper basket. This attitude undoubtedly pays. A few weeks later, she came round with some books and toys from our former home in case they were of use. Learn to let go. Even if you never meet again, be reconciled in your own mind.

In many cases, you can salvage a lost friendship, or at least a reasonable acquaintance, even though getting back together would be absolutely out of the question.

More about children

Take the same attitude with the children. They have been through the storm and we should consider them a major priority, our aim being to re-establish them in a loving relationship with both parents. We should try to establish a flexible pattern. Normally, parents are admirably sensible and, quite rightly, work these matters out without the assistance of lawyers and the courts. It is trite but true to point out that an informal decision worked out by parents is almost bound to be better than any formal legal decision. You cannot legislate for the vagaries of human nature so even the best court order is inferior to sensible parental agreement. The judge may well be learned in the law, possibly quite wise. But it is *your* family and, unless your former partner is quite impossible (as they sometimes are), you should be able to work out the day-to-day details yourselves. What is more, if there are some difficulties, make certain that you are advised by fair-minded family, friends or solicitors. It is not unknown for delicate situations to be worsened by lawyers whose whole attitude seems dominated by scoring points against the other side and increasing their fees.

Flexibility, tolerance, give and take are what matter. If he brings the children back half an hour late from time to time, so what? If she alters the weekend rather late in the day (and she was always like this) so what? The happiness of the children is what matters rather than your temporary inconvenience. Of course, if such tolerance is abused then you may have to go to law and, with some difficult parents, the sooner firm boundaries are defined, the better. But, on the whole, sort it out yourself.

Concerning contact, the older the children, the more the choice is theirs until, as teenagers, their decision is final. At this time, particularly if the children are living away from you, try to keep up contact, however painful it may be. This needs restating because if you let contact lapse at this crucial time and then try to restore it many months later, you will find it very difficult, perhaps impossible, and both you and your children will be the losers.

A plea to older children

Let me say at this point a word to older children directly. When your parents first divorce it is not surprising that, because they are in difficulties, they may well say things about the other parent which should not be said. One or both of your parents may have behaved very badly. All the same, try hard to form your own independent relationship with each of your parents. Your parents' quarrels are not your quarrels.

I recently read in a magazine a corrosive article by a young woman whose parents' marriage had recently failed. In it she stated that she intended to have nothing further to do with her father who had run off with somebody else. I don't know all the facts but I question whether this attitude will, in the end, do either her, her mother or her father any good. And when she comes to marry, what about her husband and her own children? This is not a wise long-term solution.

In one extreme case, the 'bad' parent died whereupon one of her children, well into middle age, said very bitterly, 'I will never forgive her.' So far as I know she still hasn't but the effect on her is clearly not good. Your parents' quarrels are not your quarrels.

Don't outlaw the in-laws!

Talking to parents again: as far as possible, try to rebuild links with your in-laws. If they have been the main cause of the trouble, to your mind, this may not be easy. But very often, the grandparents have been most distressed by the separation and should be forgiven if, from time to time, they have over-reacted or have supported their own child against you. Put yourself in their shoes. After all, you and I would probably do the same. It is only natural to support one's own children to the outside world. We may well disagree with them in private whilst supporting them in public. Now that you are separated remember the difficulties they faced and also remember that, probably, they heard only one side of the truth. It is far better to re-establish contact with them, if you have children. If you do not have children, this may not be necessary.

So often, grandparents have an affinity with their grandchildren which is lacking between parent and child. Grandparents often have the time and the wisdom which we parents lack. Genetically, half of our child's heritage comes from each side. In fact, one side may well turn out to be more dominant than the other. Your husband's father may well have more to offer your son than your own father, just because he likes fishing whereas your father prefers books. My mother-in-law has always had far more understanding and affinity with our daughter Harriet, now 12, than my own mother. My own mother was always kind and interested but was not on the same wavelength. This happens in all families. For your children's sake, foster this relationship, see that they remember birthdays and festivals and encourage visits and telephone calls, even if, for a while, you find it too painful to be closely involved.

The same principles should apply to certain valuable old friends, though you may rightly decide that some friendships are beyond recall. From your point of view, this may be true, but not necessarily from your children's. Unless you consider the friendship undesirable, it may be as well to continue it, even on a less intense level, for the sake of your children. As for yourself, you have many years in which to forge new friendships. One can still make new friends at 80!

Challenges

Now is the time to get involved generously in challenges which will take you out of yourself. During the separation, you probably lacked the time, the will and the energy to do this. Summon up your willpower, take your courage in both hands and attempt something different, even difficult.

An excellent start is to dig out your old address book and work through it. You may well find, as I did, that you don't recognize some of the names and addresses at all! I will be surprised, however, if it doesn't produce some leads. At this time, most of us need to rebuild our confidence. If only there were confidence classes easily available. All the same, with help from friends or family, you could throw a small party. This need not be expensive. As students, some of us gave a lunch party every Saturday but the rule was that our friends brought what they could. If rich, they brought drink. If poor, they brought bread. If in the middle, they brought fruit or cheese. Amazingly, it all worked out very well.

In contrast to this, a friend, recently separated, wrote: 'I found it very healing to be with people I'd never met before.'

I understand both points of view. Perhaps the answer is to have a go at both, resurrecting your old friends and finding new friends.

It is not a question of money, which may well be in very short supply. It is far more a question of looking confidently to the future, saying to yourself, 'Well, what have I always wanted to do or see or learn or become?'

I know a woman who faced the death of her two young sons from a wasting disease. She was then divorced and found herself utterly alone. When I met her she was running an old people's home, pouring into the old people all the love and energy that she had. A remarkable achievement.

Alex Torbet is a murderer serving a life sentence at Saughton Prison, Edinburgh. His advice is being sought by scientists and academics the world over because he has become internationally known for his ability to breed fish. Apparently his work may play a part in freeing people in the Third World from hunger. In my files, I have many stories of people who have helped themselves get over the death of a child, a partner or a friend by pouring themselves into a cause or a challenge. A quiet example comes to mind. An elderly man works in one of our local cancer charity shops. He is there every day, on the till, always helpful and friendly. One day, although I had guessed the answer already, I asked him why. 'Simple,' he replied softly, 'my wife died of cancer. I didn't want to be a burden to my children although they are very good to me, so I started to help here.' He helps but is himself helped, as he would be the first to agree.

These examples make the point that people faced with almost overwhelming problems can, with courage, triumphantly overcome them.

And forgiveness again. Some years ago, the flavour of the month was Canadian Air Force exercises. The idea was that, whatever your age and health, if you practised them 11 minutes a day, your health would radically improve. Many of us tried, only to fall by the wayside a few weeks later. But the principle was undoubtedly correct. Every day, you exercise. Every day, little by little, you become healthier. Likewise with forgiveness, so forgive daily. Practise each day.

Forgiveness is a decision not a feeling. Let me repeat that. Forgiveness is a decision, not a feeling. It is an act of will. You *decide* to forgive. Here a little, there a little. Begin with small gestures, begin by forgiving small things, gradually moving to the fundamentals. In plain human terms, whatever your religious beliefs, remember that if you continue to blame your former spouse for your troubles this will stop you from rebuilding your own life. You will continue to feel like a victim and you will be letting your past taint your present and your future. Your aim should be to be reconciled with your partner. By this, I do not mean reconciliation by returning to live together (though it would be wonderful if this were to take place). What is intended is a feeling of reconciliation such that you no longer harbour any bitterness. This may take a long time, but it is well worth striving for.

Why not try and bring to mind the good things in your relationship? It may have ended badly and sadly but it wasn't always like that, so why let the last few years or months ruin what went before? A good friend recently wrote, 'I cannot for a moment have any regrets, because there were years of happiness together and three unrepeatable children.' I entirely agree. All of us should have some happy memories to fall back on and, in most cases, including mine, the happy memories far outweigh the bad.

Some months ago I inherited a jumble of family photographs, mainly taken in the Isle of Wight. The photographs were hardly professional, in some cases they were downright bad – but the picnics, the sand castles, the tears, the laughter were all there. Proof positive which I have never doubted that for many, many years my first marriage was happy. Don't let the end destroy or taint those memories for too long, although naturally enough, in the early days of separation it will be hard to have this point of view. Only when all these matters have been substantially settled, should you consider a new deep relationship.

How to help

What about the helpers? Are they still needed or can they retire gracefully? Without doubt, they are still needed, and in many ways their help may well be more important now than before. The reason is that when people are splitting up everyone is keyed up, well aware that Jane's divorce is coming up in March or Tom's sorting the money out in April. At that time, the victim not only has personal help, but also professional help which, if the matter has been going on for a long time, may well also verge on the personal. All these dealings have a high profile and then, as pointed out above, the decree absolute or the separation agreement is an anticlimax and there is an understandable tendency on the part of the helper to consider that the job is done. But it isn't. The victims may well be less vocal about their problems. There may well be less involvement with the other side or with lawyers and the courts. But they are still in a most vulnerable position and still need your help, even if it is hard for them to ask for it.

Remember this: that most of us get a good deal of our sense of personal identity and fulfilment from our family roles and sometimes from our work roles. Each of us is an individual, then a couple and then a family, and when we lose our role as a couple and our role in the family is radically altered against our will, we feel very lonely and exposed. We need all the help we can get, but we may be too proud or shy or played out to ask for it.

In the early days, when there was a children's hearing, quite understandably a worried parent might well ask you to come along to give moral support. So you would reschedule your diary and go. Six months later, although there is no court hearing, the same parent is still very anxious about seeing or not seeing the children and still wants to talk over problems with you. They may well not ask, so you will just have to telephone or drop by just to 'see how things are'. Life can be very bleak after the collapse of a relationship, even if that relationship was not particularly happy. The 'suddenly single' are very vulnerable and outsiders, once the dust has settled, tend to forget this. There is a black hole, an emotional vacuum. Those with children probably have too much to do. Those on their own probably have too little to do. Either way, as helpers, we can get involved.

The reality is that the victim is older, battle-scarred, and still convalescent. Practically speaking, their circumstances may well have changed radically. A few years ago, a man on a good income might have been living in a nice house, with two cars and three children. Now, having missed promotion, he has the same income but more responsibilities: he is living in a small two-bedroomed flat, with a smaller car, enjoying access to two of his children whereas his youngest daughter is being very difficult, wrongly thinking the divorce is all his fault. If a woman, it is very likely that she is living in a smaller house, probably in a different place, facing up to the fact that her income has dropped radically. Her children are not all that easy and she is certainly not getting any younger. The first few months, even years, after separation are very tough and the future happiness of both parent and child may well be determined by what happens in this period of transition.

As helpers, we should be discreetly in the wings. It would be unwise, even impertinent, to be too closely involved, because people must learn to stand on their own feet, unless there are exceptional circumstances. On the other hand, if you are not involved at all, the victim may well feel even more deserted than ever.

The victim is isolated and we want to show that there are other human relationships worth pursuing and developing before any new, deep emotional relationship is considered.

So hang in there!

Easier for men

It has to be faced that life for a man under these circumstances is almost always easier than for a woman. Usually the mother has the children, so her social life is considerably restricted. Furthermore, she may well have missed working for many years and, when seeking employment, she may well find that she has to be retrained. What is more, she will have the perennial problem of who is to keep an eye on the children now that the father is not available. Whatever the background, these problems are very hard to handle.

The man, on the other hand, is considerably freer. He does not have the daily pains and pleasures of his children. He has probably worked throughout the relationship and even if his career has suffered he is still capable of earning his living. Furthermore, provided he doesn't sink into self-pity or drink and the like, he will be surprised to find how eligible he is. I am not suggesting that remarriage is an answer to all problems. Far from it. But a single man, with limited family ties, is far more able to rebuild his life than is a woman with dependent children. This is an almost insoluble problem and we should try to mitigate its harsh effects as far as we possibly can.

ELEVEN

New Relationships

Statistics have been likened to a drunkard leaning against a lamp-post in that they are often used for support rather than illumination. Apparently second marriages have a less than 30 per cent chance of surviving five years or more, whereas third marriages have a less than 15 per cent chance of surviving five years or more. Whether or not you accept the validity of these figures matters little. What is quite clear is that remarriage is not a soft option and, unless handled with care, can well lead to tears – so don't rush.

A tale of two marriages

Let me begin with two friends whose stories are true and have much to teach us. Both married comparatively young, both had children. Both marriages ended against their wishes. They were very upset, as were their children, but all in all, they had behaved with reasonable dignity and common sense. The future was relatively hopeful.

Then their paths began to diverge and, many years later, the seeds sown in those early years after divorce have grown into mature plants. One friend was determined that no serious new relationship would be considered, let alone started, until as many as possible of the loose ends of the first had been tidied up. Thus, strenuous efforts were made to tie up the finances, to sell the house, to resettle the children, the whole idea being to make as clean a break as possible.

In contrast, the other friend, against all rhyme or reason, embarked on a new, intense relationship even before the divorce was finalized and before any of the loose ends were tied up at all. The matrimonial home was not yet sold, the maintenance was not yet sorted out, the children were still deeply unsettled when the friend and his new partner decided to live together only a few miles down the road.

The result? Inevitably, the first friend fared much better than the second. In the first case, after the divorce a reasonable, even friendly, relationship was established between all concerned, to the considerable benefit of the children. When this friend later remarried, everyone co-operated. As to the other, the wrangling continues to this day. One painful result is that the children of the first marriage have never seen, let alone become friendly with, the children of the second marriage. How very sad. Particularly if we remarry later in life, our children have all the more need of their older half-brothers and sisters.

As you have no doubt found, if you yourself are divorced, people tend to share their own experiences with you. Thus, certain common points emerge which are well worth considering.

Take it slowly

The first principle is, don't rush. Don't rush into another relationship before you have recovered from the trauma of the first. Perhaps this analogy may help: every year in the London

Marathon many runners, both amateur and professional, run through London, raising money for charity. The event has become increasingly popular. You have to be fit to run in a race and very fit indeed to run in a marathon. You have to train, controlling your food and drink and exercising regularly. If you don't, not only would you not complete the marathon but you might damage your health, even fatally. Human relationships are like a marathon. In our first marathon, whether our fault or not, we stumbled and fell. We needed doctors and nurses to patch us up and, even now, have not fully regained our former fitness. How silly to enter another marathon before we've recovered from the first.

Another way of looking at it is to consider scar tissue. Your separation has left you with scar tissue and you must let this heal properly, otherwise there is a high chance that you will knock the scab off the wound or wounds and the whole healing process will have to start all over again. (I trust doctors will forgive me if, medically, these details are not quite correct!) The point is that you must let your emotional wounds heal, working through the grief process until you feel strong again. This is a counsel of perfection which few of us can attain. Right at the end, a new relationship can of course complete the recovery, but try to recover as much as you can before undertaking this new relationship.

In practical terms, this entails sorting out as many residual problems as you can. Loose ends, like flaying ropes on board ship, can trip you. These loose ends may not be directly connected with your former marriage. They may also entail getting your private finances, as far as possible, into a more healthy shape. Likewise, your health. While going through a divorce, you may have started drinking or smoking too much. Now is the time to tackle these problems. In short, you must attempt to put your house in order.

It has been said that to unbond from a first mate takes one

year of healing for every four years. By rule of thumb, I agree with this principle which, I believe, comes from America. Don't be depressed by it if you have been married for many years, because I dare say that, by the time you are reading this book, you will be quite well into the healing process. Either way, have it at the back of your mind that the longer your relationship, the longer you need to recover from its breakdown. It's plain common sense.

Living with who you are

Leading from this, we come to a second important principle, which is learning to live with yourself. George Bernard Shaw once said that the one golden rule is that there are no golden rules. I disagree. Before you consider a serious new relationship, the golden rule is that you must learn to live with yourself, as an independent individual. I found this very hard to do. Going from boarding-school to university to sharing digs in London, followed by ten years of happy marriage, I was singularly ill-equipped to live on my own. Over forty, I found that my friends were nearly all married. I hadn't had to cook or wash or iron for many years – not that I hadn't pulled my weight in my first marriage because, in fairness to myself, I consider that I had. All the same, the temptation to avoid some of these problems, both practical and emotional, by living with somebody else was very strong indeed.

I am so glad that I did not. With hindsight, I find it was very valuable indeed to have the time and opportunity to work out or attempt to work out where I was going. Most of us, once launched on a relationship and our career, never stop to give ourselves time to think. We save this up for retirement, which is often far too late. As the poet W. H. Davies puts it so well, 'What is this life if, full of care, we have no time to stand

and stare?' Once you can live with yourself, warts and all, you stand a very much better chance of living successfully with somebody else.

Was it Don Juan who said that marriage is like a besieged city? Those married inside it want to get out whereas those outside it want to get in. Many single people imagine that if only they had a partner their problems would disappear overnight. How very wrong they are. There is considerable pressure in always being with someone. Personally, I consider that it is all worth while (most of the time!), but the joys of being single should not be forgotten. To have complete control of one's money, one's time, one's life is not to be sneezed at, even allowing for periods of loneliness and frustration. These are all matters which deserve serious consideration as you learn to live with yourself.

From recent discussions with single people, I am sure that it is vital to have a positive attitude to single life. I think of three friends. All are single, all would like to settle down with a permanent partner but so far this has not happened. Two of them plan their lives positively. They tackle both their work and their play resolutely, planning their evenings and weekends and holidays with great care. They are always fun to have around, however they may be feeling. The third friend is now less of a friend. Desperately anxious to settle down, her increasing unhappiness puts people off and, as an outsider, I cannot help feeling that she has wasted many years in regretting her single state instead of making the best of it. Ironically, if she complained less, she might have found a permanent partner. This can happen to men, but less often, because even nowadays men are more socially mobile than women. If they really want to, men can probably find a partner rather more easily. Unfair but true.

Once you are through this transitional period and have decided that you would like to settle down again with somebody else, may I suggest that you take into account some points which, in the happy heat of the moment, you may well overlook.

The effects of age

An obvious point. Your potential new partner is very likely to be older than first time round. Life may well have taken its toll.

In addition, being older, we will both lack the youthful resilience, the sheer energy, which in earlier days just carried us through problems, at least for a while. So, objectively, as far as you can be objective in the affairs of the heart, it is a good idea to examine yourself and each other before the matter gets too serious.

The effects of children

Children and stepchildren are considered in the following chapter. Remember that one of the main causes of failure or difficulty in new relationships is the effect of the children. Children almost always remain loyal to their own parents and will, time and time again, cause trouble for step-parents. It is only natural for us to feel closer to our own children than to others'. If you are going to set up a home, both of you bringing children to the family, there may well be conflicts of loyalty. These conflicts can be resolved but it is glib thinking not to anticipate them before you embark on a new relationship.

Furthermore, never underestimate the trouble which older children can cause. Whatever their ages, some children can be plain difficult once their parents find someone else, even if the parents separated many years before and even if the parent is seeking to live with somebody totally unconnected with the breakdown of the first relationship. On one view, these children, once they have left the nest, should consider that their parents' lives are no concern of theirs. On the other hand, our parents are always our parents and, particularly if we are rather vulnerable ourselves, we can be disturbed by new relationships even if adults ourselves.

I can think of at least one instance when a child, grown up and professionally qualified, determined to make the parent's new marriage founder. The effort failed, but not before considerable lasting damage had been done.

Needless to say, these points are not meant to alarm you. But they are worth considering, as is the status of the person you are thinking of marrying.

If single

If your new partner has not had a serious relationship before, they may well not be used to the hurly-burly of family life. The happier someone's childhood with the benefit of brothers and sisters, the less of a problem there is likely to be in later life. All the same, your intended partner may have had no real intimate contact with children whatsoever and will, quite justifiably, lack that rapport or touch with children which most of us have, to some extent, once we have children of our own. If this is so, there is all the more reason to take the relationship slowly; and very slowly indeed with your children. They have lost their father, so they may well find a potential stepfather very threatening. They may well misbehave and he, in turn, will be uncertain of how to react. Does he take such misbehaviour seriously or does he attempt to laugh it off? If he had children of his own he would probably know instinctively which course of action was better.

Years ago, in the grand days of Hollywood, I enjoyed a film which explored this problem. The father fell in love with a beautiful younger woman. His children quite deliberately put her through her paces and, quite convincingly, showed the father that she was quite unsuited to family life. This being Hollywood, he promptly reunited with his wife and they all lived happily ever after! While some childless people have an innate ability to get on with children, some, nice as they are, just can't get it right.

If widowed

Your intended partner may have been widowed. The crucial question is, has he or she recovered sufficiently?

Those widowed should mourn their dead and, if they wish to start again, then concentrate on the living. It is vital that they well and truly bury their dead before contemplating a new relationship. Sadly, some people cannot do this. They are always harking back, which makes a new relationship very hard to handle. A variation on this theme is admirably explored in Daphne du Maurier's novel *Rebecca*. Rebecca, the first wife, is dead but the husband seems haunted by her, thereby seriously endangering his second marriage. Fortunately, once this ghost is exorcised, the second marriage flourishes and the book has a happy ending.

It is unhealthy when people are continually referring to their dead partner, thereby making a new relationship almost impos-sible.

At the same time, it is only right that those who take on the widowed should allow some space for memories of the past. It is quite artificial for no mention of the past to be allowed. The first relationship should be mentioned, quite naturally, from time to time. Moreover, even when you are happily together

many years later, there may well be short times when your partner should be allowed privacy for memories. For example, if
the first partner died at Christmas, the very festivities may
bring back the memories, or the death of parents or particular
relatives or friends may well be very poignant. Within limits,
they should be allowed to experience these memories in peace.
It is all a question of balance.

The past can be very tenacious. I have never forgotten a
wedding I attended many years ago. The father of the bride
had been dead for over twenty years, and the mother had been
most happily remarried for many years and had had other children. However, at her daughter's wedding this mother was
almost overwhelmed by grief at sudden unexpected memories
of the dead father. Mercifully, walking around the churchyard
with the sun shining and people laughing, we were able to
discuss this so that her family never knew. In fact I am sure
that her new husband would have understood.

If divorced

Finally, your new partner may have been divorced. Without
suggesting that this book has all the answers, because it
plainly hasn't, I would suggest that unless you are reasonably
satisfied that your new partner has recovered, you should be
cautious. It may well be just a question of time. You may have
to say something along the lines of, 'Look, I would love us to
become far more deeply involved than we are but, for the
moment, I am sure you have got things to sort out so why
don't we cool it for a while?' This is easier said than done, but
if you don't say it you may well have to pay a heavy price later.

Only a few months ago, a friend began to fall for somebody
who had not quite recovered from her divorce. It was very

painful to see a potentially fruitful relationship end when, who knows, had they waited a little while, something permanent might have come out of it.

TWELVE

Stepchildren

An estimated three million children will be growing up in step-families by the end of this decade, that is a quarter of all children born. At the moment, there are at least six million people who are part of a step-family in this country. What is more, those very families will be interconnected with other families, so you are bound to meet this question, directly or indirectly.

Unfortunately, there is a tendency to marginalize step-families and their particular problems: 'Jane's got a new boyfriend … I think he's got two kids but they live with the mother.' Do they indeed? They are still his children. They are part of the package, or so they should be. So how are they going to get on with Jane? And how is Jane going to get on with their mother, and how is everyone going to get on if they have children of their own, or if their mother has children by a new partner who has, himself, got children already? Make no mistake. This is a very deep and difficult subject. If you are experiencing problems, you could always contact the National Step-Family Association. Their telephone number is listed at the end of this book in the section on Useful Organizations.

I am not a stepfather myself but I have had two stepfathers and a stepmother and am, of course, married to a stepmother, my two children having been 13 and 11 when we married in 1983. What follows may assist with the practical details but, essentially, difficult though it may be, if we love the parent, we should try to love the children. And that parent should remember: 'Once a parent, always a parent.'

Dead or alive?

There is an undoubted difference depending on whether the natural parent of your stepchild is alive or dead. There are important adjustments to be made either way. If you marry someone who is widowed you must always respect the children's memories of their dead parent, at the same time making discreet allowance for rose-tinted spectacles. (Indeed, so many 'perfect' people die daily according to their obituaries that I am amazed the world goes on without them.) Seriously, you must accept that you can never replace the dead parent, and the children must always be given space, a niche for that parent's memory and influence.

The older the child, the more the space. Thus, if you take on the child when an infant, your influence will be proportionately greater. Even so, if you are usually called 'Daddy' or 'Mummy', the child should be told the truth when older. If reasonably possible, you should encourage contact with the dead parent's family. They may well have much to contribute both practically and emotionally, particularly if you go on to have a family of your own. Incidentally, while it is useful to find out the truth about the dead parent, it is probably not wise for you, the step-parent, to tell the truth to the child. If home truths have to be told it would be better to persuade someone else to tell them. For example, if the child is saying that his late mother rivalled Mother Teresa in sanctity and you know that the opposite is the case, try hard not to let the truth slip out unless absolutely necessary. It will only confuse the child.

Different standards

Generally, the other parent is alive and possibly kicking, and the children may well think that you are trying to replace their true parent. It is very difficult when your standards are totally different. You are teetotal whereas Tom's father is alcoholic. An insoluble problem, but love, fortified by humour, can help considerably. When your stepchildren are under your roof, you are entitled to expect them to honour your way of doing things. In short they should respect you and your standards. If they have to be disciplined, then their own parents should do this except on rare occasions. At the same time, just as your husband should be scrupulously careful not to be rude about his former partner to the children, you should be even more scrupulous.

More optimistically, why not try hard to establish working relationships all round? Believe me, this can be done, and in my own case, I am genuinely grateful to my former wife and to my present wife, who from the very start, have always got on well together, thereby making our children's lives much easier and happier. This advantage has blessed not only the older children but also the younger ones, who occasionally visit my former home and enjoy doing so, provided that biscuits are on hand and the dog is kept under control.

At times, the objectivity of the step-parent who is involved, yet not too emotionally involved, can prove quite invaluable. During one crisis I well recall that my present wife and my former wife's husband were far wiser about our son, then a teenager, than either of us natural parents. Ironically, we parents had to agree with their assessment.

Sadly, far too often the new partners can take on their partner's old quarrels with a vengeance. If the new partner was involved in the actual break-up then this attitude, although regrettable, is understandable. But if they were not, it is very unfortunate. There is a fresh chance of forming a working relationship. So if the parents are not able to do this, then it is all the more important for a step-parent to try to be a go-between. Sometimes it is out of the question. 'He ran off with her in the first place, how dare she collect David from school?' As time marches on, this attitude can and should soften for the sake of the children, and many a potential court case has been resolved by the quiet help of a discreet step-parent.

From April 1992 to May 1997, Gillian Shephard had a seat in the Cabinet. No mean achievement. Years ago when she was 35, she married a widower with two children aged 11 and 14 and gave up her job to look after them. Writing in the *Independent* newspaper she explained how a close friend told her, 'Never forget you can't be their mother, but you can be their very best friend.' What wise advice! 'You can't be their mother but you can be their very best friend.' If only more people realized this, there would be much less tension in many a household, as more and more people separate and form new relationships, bringing their children with them. Mrs Shephard goes on to say, 'I have always treated them as equal and as individuals – rather than extensions of myself as parents often do.' Her stepson, Neil, then 26, showed how well she succeeded. 'My overriding memory of my step-mother is one of fun and humour. There was no threatening scenario because she wasn't a replacement and she never tried to be my mother. She tried deliberately to be my friend. She was always very encouraging ...'

The difficult child, the difficult partner

What do you do if the stepchild is impossible? This may not happen, but if it does then we have to remember our priorities. Love partner, love children. Now that you have a new relationship your duty is to love your partner. Your new relationship must come first, and always remember that although the difficult child is only on loan to you for a few years, your new partner is there for life, or should be. While every effort should be made by both of you to love and cherish the difficult child, in the end your marriage comes first. Some children, even quite young children, quite deliberately and maliciously set out to wreck a new relationship, wishing to keep their parent for themselves. It may take months, even years for a workable harmony or equilibrium to be achieved. Persevere, but in the final analysis your relationship comes first.

Without going back on this at all, it is prudent, particularly in the early years of a new relationship, to allow your spouse to have some space in which he can maintain, even develop, his relationship with his own child. Both parent and child need this, although over the years you may become increasingly part of the scene. Thus, if he likes football why not encourage him to take his son to see a football match, just the two of them, while you have an afternoon at home, ending up with a splendid meal for all three of you? If he were your own son, you might well do this anyway. So there is no need, out of a sense of insecurity, to insist on going too.

We all know of cases where, for no good reason, step-parents have banned children from the home, so that either the children have lost all contact with their parent or they have had to continue the relationship in an underhand way. What an indictment of you if he can't honestly say, 'I am taking Tom out for a drink this evening,' rather than, 'Sorry I'm late, I had a tough day at the office.' We know one person whose integrity we value considerably. None the less, such is the relationship between his new partner and the stepchildren, that lies have to be told when these children are seen. 'White lies' are still lies and this surely can't be good for the new relationship.

The wicked step-parent

Nowadays, it is quite usual to find mother with her children, father with his children (visiting from time to time), coupled with a child or two of the new relationship. Although very hard work, this can be great fun or a total disaster. Much will depend upon your attitude. If there is a golden rule, it surely must be, 'Be fair.'

Fiction apart, there are still wicked stepmothers and stepfathers about. A woman recently wrote, 'I had the classic stepmother myself. She would never let me and my father be alone in the room together and if my mother's name was mentioned she'd burst into tears.' Of course, children's demands vary with their age and personality and, as parents, we should do our best to meet those demands, at the same time trying to be fair to all. Your one-year-old can bawl more loudly than your thirteen-year-old. Both have needs, albeit different. The baby has an immediate need to be fed or have its nappy changed. Your teenager may need half an hour's undivided attention, although she is far too proud or truculent to put this into words. Somehow or other (I often fail) you have to be all things to all children. Joshua (then 22) wanted to discuss art. Emily (then 20) wanted to discuss university entrance. Harriet (then seven) wanted me to admire her painting. Rupert (then five) wanted to do a puzzle. Benjamin (then 12 months) just wanted a cuddle. Well, try to be fair!

The wider family of the step-parent have a role to play, although far too few play this role at all generously. However,

I was recently encouraged by the story of a man who decided to invite all his grandchildren to spend a holiday with him abroad. One of his children had recently remarried, thus gaining two stepchildren. The grandfather insisted on inviting these two children, at his expense, to join this family party. Admittedly well-off, he made the gesture which must have reaffirmed and encouraged this new family enormously. Would that this example were followed more often: I repeat, it is not a question of money. It is a question of concern, encouragement, involvement, of making people feel that they belong.

Making a will

Ending on a sombre note, be fair in life and fair in death. Whatever their ages, your children are still your children. William Shakespeare, by his will, left his wife, Ann Hathaway, 'the second-best bed'. Over 350 years later, I winced on hearing how a middle-aged friend of ours, recently widowed, had been left one dining-room table by her father, who had left all his estate to his young daughter in her early twenties. When you die, try to distribute whatever assets you have fairly between your children, making due allowance for any special needs they may have. This is difficult. Opinions vary. If you have two daughters and one has children and the other hasn't, should you leave your money equally to your two daughters, or leave your estate in three parts, one third to each daughter and one third to the grandchildren? One daughter would say yes and the other would say no.

To my mind, it would not be fair to leave everything to your 18-year-old son by your second relationship and nothing to your 30-year-old son by your first relationship. There may be exceptional reasons, but at least start with the principle of equality. Not only is your elder son denied his birthright but, more importantly, he may well feel a sense of bitterness. We should strive to be parents until the day we die. As parents, in our inner hearts we may well love our children differently or we may not like them at all equally. All the same, unless there are special circumstances, it should be our duty to treat them equally.

Fiction has not been kind to step-parents, particularly step-mothers. Most of us have been brought up with the story of Cinderella. Her stepmother was bad news, as were her step-sisters, but incidentally, why on earth didn't her father do something about it? Many of us have seen and enjoyed Walt Disney's *Snow White and the Seven Dwarfs*, with its vivid picture of the wicked queen, the stepmother. Fortunately, there are many examples where, for many years, step-parents and stepchildren have enjoyed a rich and rewarding relationship. In rare instances, it can be as rewarding, if not more rewarding, than a normal parent/child relationship because some of the emotional tensions involved in the latter are lacking. Only the pleasure remains. The more you invest in this relationship the better your return.

THIRTEEN

Divorce/Separation Seminars – A Suggested Outline

Running a series

We hold seminars twice a year, in spring and autumn, meeting on four consecutive Monday evenings. The need is so urgent that an annual course would not be sufficient and, at the moment, we do not have the time or energy to run more than two a year. What about the intervening period? After our first seminar, quite a few of us felt that we had deserted some of the people who came. This is because, after weeks of rather intense relationships, the seminars ended and we all went home leaving them high and dry. This worried us. Our present solution is two-fold. First, some of us are always available informally. Second, we suggest fortnightly fellowship meetings which people may care to join. The particular fellowship we recommend is not exclusively a divorce group, but it does contain leaders who have themselves been separated. We have found that these two methods help keep people afloat in the intervening months.

One of the limitations of modern life is that the race relations industry, for example, always sees all problems in race relations terms. Socialist politicians and Conservative politicians are the same, always seeing in Socialist or Conservative terms. We are not just black or white, rich or poor, divorced or married. We are many-faceted, with much potential. Therefore, as far as we possibly can, we always encourage those we meet through our seminars and elsewhere to put their experience behind them and enthusiastically to join the wider world. This is most important. Don't let yourself be trapped in a divorce/separation ghetto, or a ghetto mentality.

Returning to our seminar series, although people are free to come and go over the four weeks, we try to encourage people to attend all the evenings. People who are tentatively forming some rapport with a helper are naturally disappointed when that helper does not turn up the following week. It takes time for relationships to form and for a sense of fellowship to develop, but we always welcome anyone who wants to come and, particularly with people whose family commitments make regular attendance difficult, always stress that we can catch up on the details at another time.

I am always amazed, having faced the audience on the first night, by how much the same audience have relaxed by the last night. Time and time again, the most unlikely people have struck up a friendship, although on occasions we have made specific introductions. Beware of typecasting people. You may have an army officer as a helper and an out-of-work labourer as a victim. In human terms they have very little in common, but since both their wives committed adultery, you may well find that they speak the same language. Likewise, as any family support group for Alcoholics Anonymous will confirm, two women dealing with alcoholic husbands have very much in common. Let them find each other out if you can, although on occasions you may have to break the ice on the lines of 'Alice, do meet Jane – she knows only too much about violence.'

Throughout, we always try to remember that we are all in this together. In a sense, we are all helpers, we are all victims.

A suggested timetable

This timetable has evolved from trial and error. We may well alter it again and, no doubt, you will have different ideas. In fact, for some years we had five evenings not four. My advice is just do it. Do something. Gather a few friends and acquaintances together, stick a notice up, phone around and adopt and change the details as you go along. What follows are suggestions, not rules written in stone.

6.30 p.m.	Helpers meet to chat – to discuss general and specific problems. These may have arisen from the last seminar or have come up during the week. We meet discreetly in a separate room from the seminar room, leaving coffee and biscuits outside the seminar room.
7.30 p.m.	Short notes being provided, I give a talk lasting approximately one hour. The idea is not to speak *at* the group but rather *with* the group. Questions are not encouraged at this stage; the material to get through is quite extensive.
8.30 p.m.	Coffee, with biscuits, sandwiches and fruit. We provide this, thanks to some stalwart helpers, and we consider this coffee break most important, enabling us all to meet and chat informally. It is scheduled for half an hour but often continues for three quarters of an hour. On the last evening, with warning, we have a party, with food and drink.
9.00 p.m. (approx.)	We go back to the seminar room for open discussion. There are difficulties and dangers in such open discussion because a few people tend to dominate and sometimes the discussion can lose its way. Try it and see how it goes, and

always have a formula to cut things short if things get out of hand. I sometimes use 'I think I'd like some more tea, wouldn't you, Rosemary?', looking boldly at my most loyal of helpers. It always works. This part of the evening is always a venture into the unknown. Rather than frighten people whose vulnerability and dignity must always be respected, we sometimes end the open meeting quite early, allowing them to escape, then go back into smaller groups, as people want.

10.00 p.m.   Departure, people being free to go whenever they like. We try to make it as easy for people to leave as to come. Babysitters can be a hassle. We end formally at 10.00 p.m. although some of us leave later.

Note: A short questionnaire is worth considering, although this would be a little heavy if you were three friends meeting over a cup of tea! It could include such questions as:

Were the talks too short or too long?
Did you like the timetable?
Did we start too early or end too late?
Was the room okay?
Have you any suggestions to make?

People are surprisingly shy about making suggestions openly when often the suggestions are sensible and easy to follow. For example, 'Why not have disposable cups?' These forms need not be signed!

A follow-up list of useful books and addresses is a good idea, but it is even more useful if you can personally recommend certain books and organizations. It carries much more weight if you can say that you have found this book or this chapter really helpful, or if you can say, 'Here's the number of Relate. Mention me and ask for Mrs Smith – she'll put you on the right track.'

A Final Word

Why me?

A final word of encouragement to all enmeshed in divorce or separation.

Why me? I well remember asking that question: 'Why me?'

My conclusions are most tentative but, for what they are worth, the following may be of some assistance.

First, all of us have to accept that, to some extent at least, we are to blame. In any breakdown, it is never 100 per cent the other person's fault. We cannot deal with our partner's faults but we can, at the very least, deal with our own.

Second, life is unfair. Many events in life are quite inexplicable. Why should your baby die of a cot death? Why should your sister die of cancer, leaving a husband and three children? There is no complete answer and it would be futile to attempt one.

Third, there are always people in a worse position than you. Take the case of Mr and Mrs McKay, now 66 and divorced. In 1982 their son Sergeant Ian McKay was killed in the Falklands war, winning a posthumous VC. In 1989, their son Neal died of cystic fibrosis and on 10 October 1995, their son Graham also died of cystic fibrosis. After his death, his father said,

'I don't know how a father comes to terms with the death of three sons – I don't think I ever will. The only thing I can do is get on with my life, but there isn't a day goes by that I don't think of them.' They have no other children.

A few months ago Mrs Joan Wilson, whose daughter Marie was killed by an IRA bomb at Enniskillen in 1987, spoke to some friends of mine. She came across as a radiant, loving woman but the facts of her life are grim. She married Gordon Wilson in 1955. In 1956 her first child Peter was born. He was killed in a traffic accident in 1994. In 1958 her second child was born. He died prematurely after a few hours. In 1960 her third child, Julie Anne, was born. She is still alive. In 1967 her fourth child Marie was born and was killed in 1987. In 1995 her husband Gordon died of a heart attack.

In 1993, I wrote the following:

In 1969 my first son Harry died after only 36 hours. At the time, his death seemed monstrously unfair and, in a sense, it undoubtedly was.

Now, with hindsight, I am quite certain his death was one of the best things that has ever happened to me, in that it began the process of breaking me down so that, heart broken, I could begin to understand how other people felt and other people suffered. Your suffering can do the same for you. It's up to you.

On 6 March 1996, his brother Joshua was found dead in his gallery, Factual Nonsense, in Charlotte Street in London. As my wife drove us across London in the small hours of the morning, what I wrote above came into my mind. I remember thinking, 'Come on. This is ghastly, this is nonsense, there can't be anything good at all in Joshua's death – someone so brilliantly talented and maddeningly loveable.' Two years later, the wounds have still not fully healed. They never will.

However, without any hesitation at all, I can say that suffering does bring benefits, deep benefits. You join a special club. You learn through pain. You see life in a different perspective and in a new depth. This can happen to you.

Chiswick, 1998

Useful Organizations

There are many useful books, but these soon become dated or out of print, so I would strongly advise you to go to your local bookshop and see what is on offer.

Without hesitation, I recommend the two following organizations:

For relationship problems:

Relate
46 Crowndale Road, London NW1 1TP
Tel: 0171 380 1463

There are local branches so consult the Yellow Pages under Counselling and Advice.

For help with step-families:

The National Step-Family Association
72 Willesden Lane, London NW6 7TA
Tel: 0171 372 0844

Their counselling service can be contacted on 0171 372 0046.

If you need telephone help because you are desperate, even suicidal, don't hesitate to ring the Samaritans. They have local branches but this number is always available: 0345 90 90 90.